D0619783

board

board

voices from *the nervous breakdown*

brad listi & justin benton

BOOKS

Published by The Nervous Breakdown Books
Los Angeles, California
www.thenervousbreakdown.com

First Edition, 2012
Copyright © 2012 Brad Listi and Justin Benton

The views expressed in this book are those of the authors
and do not necessarily reflect those of the publisher.

All rights reserved. This book, or parts thereof, may not
be reproduced in any form without permission. The
scanning, uploading, and distribution of this book via
the Internet or via any other means without the permission of the publisher is illegal and punishable by law.
Please purchase only authorized editions, and do not
participate in or encourage piracy of copyrighted materi-
als. Your support of the authors' rights is appreciated.

Book Design: Charlotte Howard, CKH Design

Cover Images: plywood courtesy Goodtextures.com;
crowd photo courtesy Orange County Archives.
Interior tag clouds generated via Tagxedo.com.

ISBN 098-2-8598-8-0

Printed in the United States of America

This book is dedicated, with gratitude, to all the writers, readers and comment board contributors at The Nervous Breakdown.

contents

the human
race
home
kurt
vonnegut
bookstores
closing
reading
aloud
audience
writing
the rest of
your life
wasting
narrative
arc
role
models
risk
reading
self-identification
money

authors' note

This book is an act of literary collage, the contents of which are derived from comment boards on The Nervous Breakdown (TNB), an online culture magazine and literary community founded in 2006. The material herein covers the first two years of the site's existence. It is important to note that the text is not presented in chronological order, nor is it attributed. The bulk of it has been carefully rearranged, and some of it has been altered for the purposes of readability.

Should the Internet as we know it someday fade into obsolescence, or meet its end otherwise, here is a brief explanation of how TNB comment culture works as of the early 21st century:

- A contributor writes a post and publishes it online, for any and all to read.

- Readers post comments beneath the post, which nest (meaning, indent) as they accumulate.

- Causerie ensues. Rapport, digression, vulgar humor, and argumentation are common. Author participation, while not required, is expected.

Once again: It's a *community*, albeit virtual, and one of unusual vitality and intelligence. If so many Internet comment boards seem like cesspools, TNB is a wading pool—warm, clear, and, for the most part, inviting.

It is our hope that this book will serve as the first volume of a unique record of the site and its many participants, and that it will help to mark this juncture in publishing history—with its tectonic shifts, its collision of analog and digital, and the remarkable wave of anxiety, excitement, experimentation, and invention that have surfaced as a result.

Brad Listi & Justin Benton
September 2012

audience time murder

the human

fame funerals
dreams waking up

condition

destiny

fear death family boredom

happiness

mothers fathers

first memories

stupidity fantasy home

getting old existence money success

reality

powerlessness

the human

race

somewhere between women and boredom

I'd had a headache all day. All of a sudden, I couldn't speak. Not even gibberish. Nothing came out. I could think of what I wanted to say but I couldn't produce the words. Aphasia, I think they call it. I flapped my hands wildly, slapped my forehead, tried to convey to my mother that I couldn't speak, that it had something to do with my headache. I managed to push out "headlight," the closest word to "headache" I could manage.

My first memory: not being able to slide down the staircase banister, like the bigger, cooler kids could. They laughed at me, called me names. I tried not to cry. It's damn right traumatic, the first time you realize you can't do something other people can do.

Mine? Getting hit by a car, flipping in the air. Coming to on the front lawn of our neighbor's house. My mom, screaming bloody murder. I get goose pimples just thinking about it now. And, my dad—where was he?

My brother and me staring into the La Brea tar pits, both of us thinking, *What in the hell did they put in that water to make it look like that?*

It was an unbearably hot summer. The summer the Night Stalker prowled Los Angeles. I can recall trying to sleep every night with the windows locked and no central air. But which did I put to memory first, the heat or the Night Stalker?

The heat is the first thing I remember. Los Angeles — a hot, insufferable kind of hell. But it will always be home to me.

Cookies and strawberry shampoo. Fire and cloudless skies. I can still smell the bonfire burning, the sugar in the air, the good vibes. Some sadness there, too.

First memories burn bright and clear.

I can't remember anything right now. I had a fever all day yesterday. It broke late last night. I can barely remember what I had for breakfast this morning, much less my first memory.

Our red-and-black Buick 88. Red-and-black, inside and out. And for the longest time, something about that color combination made me sick to my stomach. Or at least I believed it did. Turns out I was just carsick, which was something I wasn't aware one could be. To this day, I've never worn red-and-black clothes. Have never painted with red and black, either. I try to keep my distance from those colors.

My very first memory involves a nightmare I had about the Incredible Hulk. I was three, maybe four. The Hulk was chasing me through the woods. And then out of nowhere, I wound up getting caught by some witches, who put me in a big wooden cage. The witches were dancing around a cauldron filled with boiling water, and they were going to cook me and feed me to the Incredible Hulk. And then I somehow escaped from the cage and ran through the woods before making my way over to my neighbor's house, where my best friends lived, these two little identical twin girls. And the girls took me into their garage in an effort to protect me, and then I started shoveling dog food into my mouth by the handful, and then I woke up and cried for my mom, and my mom came into the room and took me out of bed and walked me into the kitchen. She sat me on the countertop and made me a peanut butter and jelly sandwich in the middle of the night, and the kitchen, I remember, had a lot of yellow in it. Old yellow stove. Yellow fridge. Yellow light from above.

1984. I'm the Incredible Hulk for Halloween. My mother slathers my entire body in green grease paint. And the next day she spends hours— I mean *hours*— scrubbing green off the carpet and the furniture and the walls.

I was maybe four years old. I prized my Incredible Hulk action figure. One day, he went missing. Where could he have gone? My house wasn't that big. I couldn't figure it out. I thought maybe my older brother took him, but nope. Grilled my best bud, Dennis, and still no dice. The next day I see our dog, Percy, dragging his butt in figure eights around the backyard. He stops, crouches over, lets out a cry, and poops. Lo and behold, there it was, a green plastic fist jutting out from the steaming pile.

My mother dressing me up as a proctologist for Halloween.

Mine's of a road trip. I'm three years old and we're driving back to California from upstate New York. We're somewhere in the middle of Nebraska. Pink lightning zigzags across the great purple sky. Raindrops rolling down the car windows. I pick two drops and watch them race each other down the glass. Neither raindrop wins. Each veers off and merges with the other raindrops.

Falling out of a tree and cracking my head open on an exposed pipe in our backyard. My father, high at the time, driving me to the emergency room, frustrated at all the blood pouring out of my head and staining the upholstery of his Grand Marquis.

My Little Pony figurines. I'm not sure I could've made it through my childhood without them. And if I didn't have them, I wonder: Would I have somehow turned out differently?

I'm suffering from an earache. My dad brings me into the bathroom. He holds me up to the mirror, trying to calm me down from crying. The image of the two of us in the bathroom mirror, I can never forget it. I remember how my dad started laughing. I don't really know why he brought me into the bathroom, or what exactly was so funny. But that image is clear as day in my mind.

I'm climbing the brown shag-carpeted stairs of our town house, searching for them. I don't know where they are, and

I've shit myself. I'm what—three? And why am I alone at this moment? I can smell it, can feel it with every step, and for the first time I acknowledge that I've done something bad. I climb the stairs scared and worried and humiliated, muttering for my parents. That's the first thing I remember.

> I'm lost in a thick crowd in the lobby at the end of *Superman II*, and I'm absolutely terrified. I think, if only Superman were real. He could use his super hearing to locate my tiny shaking body; his super vision, to locate my family. The crowd eventually thins. I see my mom and feign nonchalance, as if I knew where they were the whole time.

>> Watching my mother behead chickens. One headless chicken runs smack into the side of the farmhouse, splattering steaming blood against the white siding. I flash a look of disgust at my mother and go inside and eat a couple pieces of leftover toast.

My earliest memory is learning that socks aren't for warming your junk. My second memory is learning that mittens aren't for warming your junk. My third memory is finding a warm drawer to curl up inside of and sleep, hidden from everyone.

Your perception of who you used to be, of family, of your original home will be colored by all the experiences you've experienced. You can never really look at it the same way twice.

Early memories, hazy and yellowing. Same as the photographs that remind us.

Abandoned places can spawn unlikely determined spirits.

I returned to my long-abandoned hometown this year. I'll never do that again. It had changed so much, and so much for the worse. All the trees I remember were gone. No kids around anywhere. Whatever my hometown was had simply disappeared.

It's impossible to return home if you've been away for too long. Not only will it change. So will you.

I always thought home was wherever they buried your umbilical cord.

Turn left at the old skating rink. Drive a good 20 minutes until you reach the waffle diner. Pass the boot repair shop and turn right when you see the cow pasture. Actually, the cow pasture has turned into an apartment complex. But there are still 15 waffle diners countywide.

I've lived in Barstow, California, my whole life. Hollywood's outhouse, as I like to call it. I left for a short time, angry and embittered. When I returned a few years later, not so angry anymore, I found myself in what seemed like a different town. Still, in many ways, it was similar to what it always was: natural, distant, ugly.

I grew up in St. Petersburg, Florida. I used to loiter outside the house where Kerouac died. I'd loaf around the Beaux Arts Gallery where Jim Morrison used to hang out and which has since burned down. Both locations symbolize the beginning of the end and the end of the beginning.

I grew up in Chicago's southern suburbs. Picking on the smallest kid until he fought back and drew blood was something to do. I was the smallest kid, of course. So one day, tired of the bullying, I decide to walk a different way home. What a journey that was, the kind you just can't find in suburbia anymore. I tracked a family of ducks, discovered a pond rich with tadpoles, climbed hills and crawled under bridges, and eventually ended up somewhere many miles from home. I had no idea where I was or how to get back. Night fell. My mom, dad, and sister eventually found me asleep under a tree.

I've always wondered what it'd be like to grow up in Nebraska.

I ran around the woods near the lake, snapping photographs of strange things. It was early winter and I had on jeans, sneakers, and an old sweatshirt. The woods were green and neon moss seemed to cover everything. I kneeled down and dipped my hands into the cold mud and sifted out jagged chunks of ice. Sun poured in through the thinning canopy and glistened off the ice melting in my hands. The waterspouts were enormous; the lightning, so close you could hear the molecules frying.

Massive panic attacks. Chronic pain. Illness. Teenage suicide attempts.

I like to think people can return home. I like to think that we can progress, can combat the axiom of small-town dreariness.

All the cultured folks pick up and move. And they don't look back. This is how the creative class maintains its form.

Sometimes our old haunts need us back.

I hate it when fantasy collides with reality. Reality wins every time. Enough of these collisions and your childhood is pretty much over.

I think a lot of American kids get bored without knowing just how deep it runs, or how exactly it happened.

I started stealing when I was a bored seven-year-old. I worshipped Robin Hood, and my mother had banned any and all candy from our household. So I took to stealing entire cases of candy bars from the grocery store. I'd slip the box under my arm, walk right past the register, and sit outside, offering candy bars to the kids passing by. Taking from the rich and giving to the poor.

Back in high school, I took to stealing CDs from our local Kmart. This was back in the golden age when record companies packaged compact discs in long, rectangular cardboard boxes. All I'd do was tear open the bottom flaps, slide the jewel cases out, and slip the CDs into my coat pocket. It worked for a while, until I got caught. I got too greedy. It was the same day that I had applied for a job at the Kmart. Had on a shirt, tie, pleated slacks, hair parted, the whole nine yards. Needless to say, I didn't get hired.

I grew up in an area infested with those giant green beetles that love running into walls like drunken blimps. My brothers and I would catch them, put them in plastic jars, then play a rousing game of Beetleball, which was essentially soccer with the plastic jar as a ball. Then we would release the beetles and see if their flight patterns were altered in any way. Sure, upon release they flew into walls and stuff, but they did that sort of thing before they were captured. So our results were inconclusive.

My adolescence was spent moored to one screen or another. Inside, most of the time. Video games. VHS. Personal computer. Hell, I used to watch at least five hours of television per day, easily.

I've read somewhere that television sets exist in 99.7 out of every 100 households.

In my opinion, you can let small children play as many video games as they want. But when they start getting better than you it's time to get them a new hobby.

Understanding the world around you is an inconvenience. But, hey, sometimes you just have to turn away from the television and take a look at things.

My only familiarity with the Japanese culture can be traced to the afternoon I defeated Piston Honda in *Mike Tyson's Punch Out*.

Who is Piston Honda? And what is *Mike Tyson's Punch Out*? I apparently have a brontosaurus-sized gap in my pop culture knowledge.

It continues on for a whole new generation of kids. All of them overstimulated in various ways. The constant barrage of electric light and sensational images flashed at them on a daily basis. All of them understimulated in various ways: emotionally, intellectually, aesthetically, socially

The thing that damages children irreparably is not knowing who their parents really are. Their mortality, that's hardly shocking.

I want my child to look around the room at my circle of friends, at all of these different people, and I want her to sense the endlessness of their personalities. If all she sees around her is an endless

variety of people, then of course that's going to make her realize
that she, too, can be endless.

> friends are
> lanterns
> through the dark

>> Yet, it's hard to transcend your DNA. I mean, me, I'm a
>> crazy bookworm just like my dad.

For several years I worked in a paperboard factory. My job
involved picking up stacks of paperboard and shoving them into
glue machines. My hands were constantly slashed up from the
sharp edges of the paperboard. The machinery was loud and I had
to wear earplugs for every 12-hour shift. I worked six days a week,
and did so for close to three years. It seemed like a lifetime.

> North American minimum-wage retail work is really no bet-
> ter or worse than getting drafted into the military at 18.

I once worked in Fergus Falls, Minnesota, as a reporter. Fergus
Falls had a pet-grooming place called Curl Up and Dye. My first
story involved a deer that jumped through the window of the Curl
Up and Dye and curled up and died. Just like that.

The smart kids not only realize what's happening to them; sooner
or later they do something about it. They seek out the good

stuff—the nourishing stuff—and band together with like-minded people. It's the only way in.

The music underground is and always was largely composed of bored, angry kids. Meantime the kids who aren't that smart—or, in any case, never had the right guidance—they go on absorbing all of the gunk. They're left behind, angry and depressed in ways they can't quite articulate.

Anger is an energy. And denial of it causes cancer.

My parents encouraged a lot of behavior most parents don't encourage.

I'm totally passive-aggressive. I'm forever irreversibly fucked-up.

I have my fair share of faults, but passive-aggression has never been one of them.

It took me too long to realize that I don't think, behave, and live like anyone else around me.

My parents definitely noticed. But as a teenager, I thought of myself as pretty typical for my age, albeit a little angrier. And what did I have to be angry about? I was bored.

It sounds sort of embarrassing to say of oneself now, but I absolutely considered myself a rebel. Still do.

I've always gone against the grain. Don't know why. There's something deeply wrong with me. I'm stubborn, right down to the bone.

When I was a teenager, my mother used to come into my room every Saturday morning at the butt crack of dawn and vacuum. When I complained, she would say, "I'm sorry, am I interrupting your laziness?"

I remember sticking Mr. Yuck stickers on inappropriate or incongruent surfaces in elementary school. My first act of transgression.

Sticker placement can be referred to as bombing or sticker bombing. Tagging is used more in regards to spray paint usage. Some people tag on a sticker to bomb with, if that makes sense.

The highest priority in any mark should be maximum visibility. If that spot just happens to be illegal, even better. It's also my intention to place messages in spots that are difficult to reach.

I left home, lived a hard and fast life at a young age. I was supposed to die young, but somehow I didn't. I was supposed to die in battle, gloriously, like Achilles. Now I feel like I'm just another leech, another cog in the wheel. Soon I think I will disappear into some far-off place, maybe Mexico. I could be happy there.

I'm a man without a generation or a home. A stranger in a strange land.

I don't have a generation and don't belong anywhere, either. I'm nobody. It's always been this way.

I look at these kids today, these Millennials, and at times I still feel human.

Today I saw this young kid punch a blind man in the face. It was terrible.

What a dick. A complete waste of copulation. An orgasm squandered.

I would have run over that fucker with my car.

I honestly wish that someone would've tripped that saggy-pants-wearing little shit and stomped his face in until a cop arrived to finish the job.

Fuck society! That's the first lesson mothers should teach their kids. Fuck it all to hell!

I think we might finally be getting somewhere.

I've never belonged anywhere. I never wanted to belong. I nearly went insane about it. I didn't have a choice. I had to flee.

Oh, how quickly our youth slips away.

I've always had the desire to transport my kids to a desert island where no one can hurt their feelings.

Am I a miracle? I've never been asked that question before. My mother probably thinks so. But she'd be the only one.

My mother is worthy of many effusive adjectives.

One time my brother slammed the back of my head through a plate-glass window. So I grabbed Mom's ceramic ashtray and smashed it over his head.

I once shoved my little sister to the ground. She was talking to a local news reporter about a rare Texas snow. They ended up not using the footage, and I am still to blame.

Once my little sister chewed both plug ends of my Nintendo controllers, and so I held her hands behind her back and tripped her so she fell face-first into the floor.

My older brother tortured me when we were young. You know, big brother stuff. Folding me up in the Murphy bed. Tying me to the coffee table. Pinning my left arm down and hitting me with the free arm. "Stop hitting yourself! Stop hitting yourself!" Worst of all, chasing me around the house with the vacuum cleaner. That vacuum cleaner light — evil eye — gives me recurring nightmares to this very day.

Some years ago, I was the best man at my brother's wedding. It was a terrible affair. For starters, the two guys whom he had brought on as groomsmen were completely wasted. I followed suit. Big mistake. The wedding took place in Wisconsin. In our drunken stupor, we thought it'd be funny to toss Cheez Doodles instead of rice at my brother and his wife as they exited the church. We ruined his tux; ruined her dress, too. At the reception, I received a ticket from the local authorities for nude water-skiing. My brother had been driving the boat extremely fast. I fell so hard the impact stripped my swimming trunks right off me. Next thing you know, the Wisconsin water police were on our ass. I was so drunk at the time I kept stumbling around and falling over in the boat, saying, "I'm from LA! If you guys don't give me a ticket I'll take you back to Hollywood and make you guys stars! I'll get you on an episode of some police show or something!"

My sister and I often discuss how much we're going to enjoy going to the beach and ogling all the young men and women in their thongs when we're in our eighties.

My adolescence was spent hating my body. What I wouldn't give to have it back now. Whatever it is I would be getting back.

My mother had a heart attack about five years ago and lost half her heart and one lung.

Getting old stinks. It's just awful. And shocking. How ugly you get when you're old, for example. I look at my face and I'm shocked at how ugly I am compared to how pretty I was. And back in the day I just took it all for granted.

I look at people when they die, in the obits. The photographs. It's the same story, so shocking. Sometimes they print a young picture and an old picture together. It's so sad that the pretty person becomes this ugly person, and then they die.

And then you get used to being invisible, too.

It always mattered a lot in our family to be pretty. It always mattered a lot to me. It was difficult to take when I got older and then old and then, finally, un-pretty. People look at you and see this generic old person. The fact that I'm fat makes it worse. I don't want to see anyone because I'm so old and fat and ugly. And I don't want anyone to see me.

As a teenager, my mother was adopted by a woman who ran a boarding house. She used to have my mom make the beds after the guests had left. But she never let my mom change the sheets on a bed that only a man had slept in. This woman used to tell my mother that she could get pregnant that way. And shortly after that, Mom actually *did* get pregnant—the traditional way. Nine months later, there I was.

I remember watching television all day, watching the towers come down over and over and over again, on this maddening instant replay. I felt deadened. And all the while, there I was, unknowingly pregnant with my first child. Life was starting just when I thought it was all coming to an end.

It happens whenever I wash the makeup off my face. I look at my reflection and always see something of Pops staring back at me. That fragile, fleeting moment of clarity you get about your blood, and what you're made of.

I have to keep reminding myself that it's okay to not want kids. I'm not my mother and I don't have to be.

> Can I tell you how angry I used to get when my mother and grandmother would tell me to calm down and act like a lady? I have to remind myself on a daily basis that it's okay to get really fucking pissed off and yell and scream and punch the wall and throw shit if I damn well feel like it.

My grandma suggests I get nude photographs taken of myself. "While you've still got it," she always says.

My son keeps a chest full of costumes. At the drop of a hat, he'll transform into any number of characters. As I type this sentence, he's just transformed into the lead singer of a rock 'n' roll band.

I remember sitting on the kitchen floor, holding my baby boy while he threw up everywhere. It was a safe place. The clean-up was easy. The sadness, harder to manage.

Babies are so gross. Like, drunk-men gross.

I was ten, taking a shower, and I projectile vomited what seemed at the time like several gallons of liquefied strawberry Jell-O. My dad, hard-ass guy that he is, didn't acknowledge the awfulness of this, and made me go to school that day anyway.

Mom could never seem to get her shit together. The birth dragged on for more than a day. Everyone got tired of waiting and went home. I stayed, you know, watched a bit, read every *Highlights* magazine in the lobby, cover to cover. Eventually, I fell asleep and woke some time well after she'd finally had my sister.

In 1972, I was pregnant, and I voted for George McGovern. I thought the world would end if he didn't win. Well, he didn't, and it didn't.

This year I lost my mom, my dad, and my aunt. In that order.

I do not feel real, have not changed, and feel like I never left. I cannot pretend anymore. I take pleasure in hiding away and worrying everyone.

> I've felt mostly broken down since March. The art of existence is not so funny anymore. I currently live with a childhood friend. My college degree hangs on my bedroom wall, mocking me. I was Employee of the Month last month, but am no longer employed. My family ceases to exist. Et cetera.

In his counseling days, my father worked one night a week as an anti-suicide man. If anyone in our small Midwestern town called the suicide hotline — our home line — it was my father's job to talk them out of it. One evening, when I was 10 or 11, I answered the phone. In the near minute between greeting the suicidal caller and yelling for my father, the man on the line shot himself.

Both of my parents committed suicide. My mom jumped off a bridge in 1994, when I was 27. My dad shot himself a few years later. I didn't hear about him until last year. We hadn't seen each other since I was five. Sometimes life is so cruel that the only thing to think is that Mom and Dad are in a better place now. I still see my mom a lot though. Walking through the grocery store. Driving down the freeway. Buying stamps at the post office.

My mom made references to dying all the time. She'd had a near-death experience during the Vietnam War, in Khanh Hoa

Province. She was about 13 or 14 years old, hiding in a sugar cane field, American troops patrolling nearby. One spotted her and threw some sort of explosive into the field. She was never sure what it was. A piece of shrapnel struck her chest. She told me she woke up in the most beautiful place she'd ever seen—a hillside, plush with flowers, awash in warm sunlight. A woman, she said, ushered her through a gate and told her, "This is the way you need to go." She woke in a hospital, screaming, pain throbbing throughout her chest. Someone performed chest compressions on her, and eventually she recovered, but was never really the same. Then, after my dad passed away, she just wanted to die. She spent the rest of her life waiting, wishing to die.

I remember something Allen Ginsberg said to me the day my mother passed away from cancer. He placed a hand on my shoulder, looked me in the eye, and said, "Hey, it's gonna happen to you, it's gonna happen to me."

I've always found the human body to be a fascinating thing. As simplistic as it may sound, everybody has one, and everyone becomes ill at some point. And there's always a story in that.

I remember the day my father's estranged father died. All that was left fit in a shoebox. This was in second grade. The death hit me hard. I'm a deeply sentimental adult now and collect whatever scraps of life I can as little reminders.

When cancer hit him, his whole philosophy crumbled. The fear tactics he'd used on America came back on him. He lay awake at night terrified he was going to hell for the people whose careers he'd destroyed. He went on a desperate search for redemption and apologized to the many people he'd hurt.

None of my father's siblings attended his funeral. Only my siblings, my brother's partner, Dad's girlfriend, her kids, and five or so of Dad's close friends. Mom didn't go. His girlfriend was not a pleasant woman, and Mom would have surely made it more miserable than it already was. I took a train from New Jersey to South Dakota. My aunt sent with me the suit that he would be buried in. It was gray, Western-styled. One of Dad's friends came to the funeral in the exact same suit. The honor guard, confused by some close-together time zones, showed up an hour late to the cemetery.

Even on his deathbed he was still a bit of a rascal.

Hey, thanks for waiting a week before telling me that Mom died! I didn't want to go to the funeral anyway! I heard that you and the doctor agreed to give Dad a rush of morphine, so as to, you know, move him right along. Yet another funeral I had no interest in attending, right? And thanks for not telling me Dad was dead for five days so you could clear all the money out of his bank accounts. Real slick! And, of course, thank you for sending me the e-mail explaining how you never wanted to see me or speak to me ever again. That was nice. I'll make sure to save it forever.

I lost my mother when I was a stupid, angry teenager. And along with her, every possibility of ever getting to really know her. For the six months prior to her death I knew I was going to lose her. Paralyzed by fear and selfishness, I could never sit down and tell her how much I appreciated her, and how much I would miss her. But, my God, how I miss her. It's beyond words. I miss being mothered so very, very much.

When I was young, I used to hold my breath whenever I passed by a graveyard. I feared inhaling the spirit of a dead person.

We reached the gravesite. I tripped on a dirt mound that had a sheet over it, nearly busting my guitar, and as the platform lowered the coffin into the hole, Grief Armageddon III was unleashed. The chain broke and the casket tipped down and stopped. We all had to wait a brutal 20 minutes until a maintenance man came and jumped up and down on the casket until the chain caught and resumed lowering. While we were waiting we took requests. After about three hymns somebody asked us to play "The Thunder Rolls." The preacher resumed the service, the blue skies went black, and it started to rain. We had one more song to go. Abe Lincoln huddled close to us and held an umbrella over our heads while we sang out "Blessed Assurance."

I buried her with my favorite guitar.

I remember the afterbirth, and my twin girls being gone. They wheel me into a small room. My husband comes in and tells me one of the girls needs AB-positive blood, which the hospital is out of. She'll get some tomorrow, he tells me. A woman comes in with a bright red lipsticked smile, hands me a pen and a clipboard, which holds the death certificate. She asks me to sign off on my other daughter's death, asks if I want the corpse for a funeral. I cannot speak. I slip out of body, looking down at the bed, at the room, the nurse. Another nurse comes in with a Polaroid of my living daughter in an oxygen tent, needles poking out of her every-where. "They look exactly alike," the nurse tells me. Her use of the present tense levels me. All of this unfolding before I can even make sense of it. I have my daughter cremated, in the basement incinerator, along with the severed limbs and tumors of strangers. I request her ashes, but the doctor tells me that the incinerator will burn everything away, including the ashes. They cart me to another room. My roommate has just had her second boy, whom she expressly hates. She had wanted a girl. Irrational thoughts of murdering this terrible person cross my mind. How would I do it without getting caught? The room fills up with expensive flowers, arranged, vased. Flowers, flowers, flowers. Sweet-smelling flowers that make me want to vomit. Eventually I go home, with my sweet, surviving daughter, a lone twin. My mother greets us. "You see," she says. "I was right. I told you you didn't need a double stroller, and you didn't listen to me. I told you I was right."

I've never understood the fear of death. I fear dying—the slow painful deterioration that leads up to death. But death itself, that's something different. That's a nonissue. I figure I'll be dead so what the hell will I care?

From time to time, in what I'd call extremely rare instances, I get the feeling that death could be authentically funny. Most of the time, though, it's pretty grim, pretty lame. And wildly uncomfortable.

I had originally picked out my own casket, but have since decided to be more frugal. I'm going to have my remains cremated so my kids can mix me into my paint set and paint me a few pictures. Of course, they can do what they want with me. If they want to keep me around and talk to me, that's fine. The way I do with my mom. She's sitting on her perch, right here in my house.

My family has always preferred open caskets.

My Uncle Steve had a mustache. The mortician, for whatever reason, covered it in makeup. Who covers a mustache with makeup?

When my mother died I wanted a closed casket. Because when my father died he looked nothing like himself. They had stuffed his mouth with who-knows-what. He looked like someone else, all odd and puffy. I didn't want to go through that again.

My brother—the golden child—wanted an open casket for our mother. I told him that I was in control of our mother's funeral, that he could go crack open the casket and steal a look if he so desired. I was the one paying for the funeral and the casket better damn well be closed if I said so. My brother later admitted that I had made the right choice about the closed casket. The mortician had placed someone else's glasses on her face. For all eternity, donning the wrong prescription lenses.

I don't mind touching dead flesh, but it's my family responsibility to make sure the corpse in the casket is lint-free.

I have a running bet with my friend Ronnie. Whoever dies first has to buy the other's headstone.

Death reshuffles the deck, refocuses one's priorities. And sometimes death makes you play 52-card pickup.

I think the word *death* deserves official proper noun status.

Whatever you do, do not delay your family for education, for money, for anything. Treasure them.

When faced with that circumstance of death and the moments before its utter inevitability—and in light of the fact that things tend to mean what we think they mean—I'd prefer to go out with a laugh instead of a whimper. I'd prefer to see life as some sort of cosmic joke that humans don't get, and then proceed from there.

My uncle used to tickle my aunt until she sobbed. Then he'd draw pictures of her crying and tape them to the ceiling where she couldn't reach them.

Whenever I complained about the snail's pace of my father's driving, he always said that if I ever had to walk someplace farther than the end of the driveway I'd really understand how big the world was.

Before I left for college, I told my dad I would eventually drop out and give stripping a try. "Where are you gonna put all those nickels?" he asked me.

Dad, he's the king of silverware balancers. "Start with a spoon," he says. I can't do it, even though I have his nose.

At least you know where you stand in the family.

The filter for our garden pond had to be cleaned. When we pulled the filter out it was filled with pollywogs. I told Dad he couldn't let them die, so he had me bring him a spoon, and we spooned them back into the pond as quickly as we could. We saved every one. I rinsed off the spoon and put it back in the drawer.

Where your father really shows off his sophistication—and proves that he truly is a man of education and distinction—is that he always purchases horseradish, and never yellow mustard.

My dad is really aware of all of the things a person can get sued for. He constantly tries to pass his legal wisdom along.

> The contents of your dad's shopping cart sound remarkably like the contents of the refrigerators of countless single adult men I've known, from college and beyond.

It soon became clear that my prudish, conservative grandfather was a serial philanderer. To the point, it seems, that he might've actually suffered from a serious addiction. Early in my parents' marriage, before all this business about my grandfather became known, a friend and mentor of my father's spent the night in their small apartment, sleeping on the couch. When my grandfather heard, he warned my parents that this was unwise. He believed the gentleman in question probably had designs on creeping into their bedroom and making sexual advances on my mother.

To tell you the truth, I've never felt like I was really a part of my family. I wouldn't say that I feel like the black sheep. I've always felt, I don't know, *adopted*. Does that make sense?

In 1991, we got a flyer, a mass-mailing job from a detective in Virginia. This detective was approaching retirement and was haunted by a case involving an unidentified murdered teenager. We were in Kentucky at the time. I can only wonder how many flyers he sent out. The only clue he had: one odd contact lens in her left eye. The officer paid for photos of the dead anonymous girl and an artist's rendering of what she might look like were she alive and had them mailed to as many ophthalmologists as possible. I painted her in oil, both dead and alive. I wanted her to know that somewhere in the ether someone was thinking about her. I still think about her. That so many years had passed and no one had claimed her is an additional tragedy that is difficult to comprehend.

> Just the thought of being kidnapped makes me shiver. I never wished for that. I did, however, dream of running away from time to time. I guess it's what happens in large families. We're just looking for a little extra attention.

Last night I dreamed that I had been kidnapped, and my kidnapper and I were driving up some old country road with a bunch of his friends. I felt exceedingly happy and free. Suddenly, the car vanished and there we were, floating up the hill, passing over some sheep and farmers. We slowly descended back down to earth. It was a blast. My ex-girlfriend suddenly appeared, grasping my arm. I played dead. Everyone panicked. She looked hard at me and saw my eye twitch. *He's not dead!* she screamed.

I had a dream of myself in my golden years, sitting on a porch swing; my son, oddly infant, suckling at my tit. Every so often, I give him a soft pat on the head and remind him not to bite so hard. He looks up at me, sleepy-eyed, and apologizes. And to that I say, "Let's not talk about love at a time like this. Who knows how long my milk will last?"

I constantly dream of trying to find a bathroom. But when I do it's always occupied and I have to go find another, to no avail.

Last night I dreamed that I had Disneyland all to myself. The entire place was completely absent of people, employees included. Except for Mickey. He was there. Imagine that.

Disneyland is best when there's no one around.

I dreamed of getting gang-raped by a pack of female bodybuilders dressed up like circus clowns.

My dreams change the tenor of my life. This can be a good thing or a bad thing.

I fly all the time in my dreams. Most of the time, I'm being chased.

I'm always disappointed when I wake up.

I woke from my dream and knew the exact day and time that I went from being a productive citizen to being a useless slob.

One of my favorite daydreams: being held at gunpoint.

I dream about beating the absolute shit out of some bulky tough guy in front of a live audience.

My dreams are like holidays. I get them once a month.

The best dreams of sleep you will ever have are the best dreams of sleep you will ever have.

> Do you get bad dreams when you drink red wine? Have I asked you this before?

>> This evening, I will have a great martini and then a terrible one. The great one should help me sleep, but the terrible one will probably keep me up all night.

Soaking listlessly in a giant hot tub filled with whole milk and Cookie Crisp at a truck stop in Mississippi. Lipping the teat of a fattened sugar hog recently liberated from a Revlon slaughterhouse. A tsunami wave of hot Crisco towers above us. In an instant, everything—the hog, the hot tub, the state of Mississippi—is gone. The crashing wave carries me away, tossing me about like a chicken wing. The Crisco subsides and I find myself at the mouth of the Karo River. I gently float along for hours under the full Moon Pie and the firmament of marshmallow stars, hearts, and clovers. Cocoa Pebbles in my hair. The river dumps me into a thick caramel sea. In the distance, I can see an oatmeal cream pie floating along, and there's someone perched upon it—a girl—flapping her arms and yelling something. I can't make out what she's trying to say, so I attempt to swim closer, with no luck, at the mercy of the dense liquid. I stop to regain my strength and decide to wait to see if the sea will somehow direct this felicitous flotsam my way. Indeed, the sea's up to something; the pie and its lucky passenger drift closer. I wipe my face clean and narrow my eyes. I can just barely make out ... Little Debbie! And as she drifts ever closer, I can hear her—she's crying out my name!

Dreams: the tossed fruit salad of our frittered minds.

I once hallucinated that everything around me was covered in a thin layer of spoiled mayonnaise.

A random Tuesday night during college. I'm all alone. For the hell of it, I take a roofie and proceed to walk around on The Hill in Boulder. I end up in a video arcade, where I play games for an hour. It takes a while for the roofie to kick in, and when it does my head feels like it's full of feathers. I experience a complete loss of inhibition. In a stupor, I shuffle over to an ice cream shop and order a chocolate gelato in a cone. I find a park bench and sit down and eat my gelato and look at the people walking by. Everybody is smiling at me. Girls are making direct eye contact and grinning at me. I feel great. I feel no pain. I think to myself, *Jesus, I must be giving off some kind of good vibe.* But, in truth, I'm missing my mouth with the cone every time I bring it to my face. Chocolate gelato all over my neck, shirt, and lap.

In my early 20s, I rode an overnight train from Marseille to Rome. My bunkmates in my sleeper car were three businessmen from China. I didn't sleep well that night. Sleeping in a sleeper car with three strangers is uncomfortable. I remember waking up early and dawn had just broken. I climbed out of my bunk and stepped outside of our little cabin. One of the Chinamen was standing there with the window open, spitting repeatedly, gutturally, forcefully. Clearing every last bit of fluid out of his system.

There aren't too many things that make me more nostalgic than acid talk.

I still dream that I'm pregnant. In one such dream, I tell my doctor I really shouldn't be pregnant, that I had a hysterectomy five years ago. To which, he replies, "Sorry, dear. It grew back."

When I was 16, I would have this dream time and again of my family's house burning down. In the dream I would try to save all six of my younger brothers and sisters, and I could save all but the youngest two. I would wake up covered in sweat and crying uncontrollably. After these dreams, I would sneak into their rooms to make sure they were okay. Then I would slip downstairs and make sure that nothing had caught on fire. Never was a fire. Never could fall back asleep.

I have this recurring dream in which I have only two kids instead of my four. We are on a dock and each toddler leaps off opposite sides of the dock. I scream for help, but no one can hear me. I cannot even hear myself. Left to decide: which child to save?

All of my dreams are crib memories.

When I was young, I was certain a robber was going to break into our house and murder me and my family.

The killers are a tandem. One holds the video camera while the other does the dirty work. They break into my house. I fight back and kick a little ass here and there, but eventually they overpower me. I try to take this in stride. After a blinding punch to the face, I tell them, "If I had wanted a kiss, I would've called your mother." My last words: "I've been stabbed harder in kindergarten!" The murder tape inevitably leaks and finds its way to YouTube, where my distraught friends are able to watch me fight for my life with great courage. One snippet—the actual moment of my expiration—becomes a popular GIF. My spirit lives on as long as there is electricity, the Internet, and YouTube.

Growing up, I was convinced that a witch lived at the end of our hallway. But she appeared like a hologram only when I was in the house, all alone. A lot of my friends claim to have been haunted by phantom witches when they were young, too.

Nothing's more frightening to a young child than realizing Mom and Dad can't always protect you.

I used to believe that all of my dolls came alive at night. I still get chills just thinking about them.

I still have this horrible fear of parking lots and parking garages at night. Those sprawling empty spaces where you scream and no one's around to hear it.

My friend Charlie and I were once held up in a parking lot. I had run the possibility of a mugging through my mind a million times before. But it went nothing like I had planned. In my imagination, things turned out in my favor. I overpowered the gunman, kicked him between the legs, did something drastic, and survived. Local news cameras swarmed me as I recounted the event a million times over. A small victory for me, but a mostly forgettable story for everybody sitting at home watching. But here's what actually happened: I handed the guy my purse and pleaded for my car keys. I don't remember what he looked like. And just like that, he was gone. Needless to say, I didn't make the news.

I knew a woman who was brutally beaten by her lover in a storage unit. He stabbed her multiple times and left her for dead. She clawed through the wall of the unit and dragged herself all the way across the lot. A night-shift worker followed her trail of blood and found her. She's alive now, thank God, but badly deformed.

Ten years ago, in Florida, a man would hide under women's cars and slash their heels as they tried to unlock their driver-side doors. I can't shake that image out of my head. In fact, now every time I approach my locked car the thought of leaping to avoid a heel-slashing crosses my mind.

A stranger's face, mere inches from yours, pitch-black dark, breathing hot, steely breaths, the knife point pressed to your neck, images of fiery skeletons dancing feverishly around your freshly dug grave—you flick on the lights and the stranger, the skeletons, all of it skitters away, a mere trick of the brain.

When I was young I thought elephants lived under my bed. Elephants that would trample me if I placed so much as a toe on the floor. I'd have to take a flying leap into bed every night. Seems so silly now, but at the time nothing felt more real than this fear.

I, too, used to take flying leaps into bed every night. I was terrified of the dark, of what lurked under the bed. I had horrible nightmares and chronic night terrors, too.

I used to lie in bed and curse God and Jesus and all the rest. I'd address him directly, whispering, "Go fuck yourself, God!" and all that. What I was trying to do was provoke God to show Himself. I wanted proof He was there. But nothing ever did happen.

You were one scary little girl.

I was one of the spooky little girls who smeared lightning bugs all over her shirt like war paint.

Women fear more not because we're irrational but because we're more often the targets.

Of females killed by a firearm, nearly two-thirds are killed by their intimate partners.

The #1 killer of African American women ages 15 – 34 is homicide at the hands of a current or former partner.

A black man is 18 times more likely to be the victim of murder than a white woman.

We're forced to acknowledge we are powerless. Our lives become unmanageable. It's much easier to split the difference, play the odds, and just stay home.

We believe that a power — a Power — greater than ourselves can restore our sanity. But we have to acknowledge that that Power either doesn't bother or is a little distracted.

The finite search. Only so much time to compile a moral inventory of yourself. It isn't pretty. Look away.

We have to admit to the exact nature of our wrongs, to ourselves, to everybody else, without fear.

I started a list of the all people I'd hurt along the way. In doing so, I learned to become willing to make amends to each and every one. I was drunk so many times and cannot remember all of the bad things I did. And the biggest mistake of all is to assume this list is finished.

When it came to death, in my mind, it was always, like, *fuhget about it.*

From out of the dampened darkness, the crickets are driven toward the light. Toward any light, really. Moving fast, searching for higher ground. Only to die in the dirt, in the weeds, right beside all the cat shit.

Oh, the mountain and its metaphors, the things it does to you, the reasons you feel compelled to climb it.

The summit is no such thing.

There is always the danger of death, my dove, chicken heart of my life. Face it. Embrace it. It will never ever go away.

The best you can do is make peace with death and toss the gnawed-up Frisbee around.

Sometime around my 30th birthday, I went through a strange metamorphosis. I started to question everything I had held to be true. Suddenly, everything I believed in turned to shambles.

I hadn't fully hatched yet when I was 22. In fact, I'm still hatching.

A corrosion of loss clots in my still unformed wings. Somewhere a woman's kiss lingers in my ghostly remains of memory.

Lately, I've been taking these long walks the way I used to take long bike rides. I'll walk for an hour every day. I walk and walk and walk, and maybe jog a little, but mostly just contemplate the whole stupid fucking universe. Because that's what it's there for. It's there for us to ponder and wonder about.

My first true awakening came about this past summer. I was at a dollar store, shopping for picture frames, and one in particular caught my eye. The insert behind the glass was a photo of a couple of models embracing each other, which the consumer was supposed to interpret as romantic love; the man, standing behind the woman, his arms wrapped around her waist, smiling smugly, looking down at— her plastic boobs? It's an abortion of a photo, with lousy models modeling real life lousily, completely unconvincing of anything genuinely human. Yet, there it sits on the shelf, unnoticed by everybody. I stood there, staring at this picture-frame insert, and I experienced a breakthrough. I realized how desensitized we really are, how dull our collective intuition has become.

I suddenly became hyperaware, and I decided I wanted to be part of some greater movement, one that counters the many images society has become so desensitized to.

I've given up on time and space and subscribe to here and now.

How sweet it is here in my American bubble with all I need.

I went through a heavy re-evaluation of everything: religion, politics, music, diet. How I wanted to live my life. It was a strange, stressful time, but it was also a very exciting time. I found a whole new person underneath the layers.

Seems to be a fairly common phenomenon.

Continue to take a personal inventory. When you are wrong, admit it.

I was heavily tranquilized and unlikely to recognize how wrong I had been.

Whatever wrong we do, we do slowly and care fully so that no one ever notices.

Maybe this is the beginning of your own metamorphosis.

Seems like I'm always becoming something.

We could all stand to be more proactive about making interesting, meaningful things happen.

I prefer a funny world. More than food, salvation, or sex, I want to laugh. That is all.

Leave it to me to find a loophole in every loophole.

"Everything happens for a reason" seems like putting the cart before the horse. We can find a reason for everything that happens to us. That's what we do: We make meaning. We are meaning-making machines.

> It can get pretty tedious, sorting out other people's meaning-making. And then, of course, our own.

Due diligence is good. But sometimes it can get in the way of having a kick-ass good time.

> Shit. I think I forgot to pay the electric bill again.

To err on the side of caution is just too damn boring.

My business partner grew a mustache when we lived in San Diego. I said to him, "You know, there are three types of people who can wear mustaches: Mexicans, cops, and gay men. You are not a Mexican and I've never seen you strapped with a pistol." He shaved it off and never grew it back. The power of honesty can change a person's facial hair forever. I all but eliminated any future mustaches from his life. You've really gotta earn that shit.

I will continue to fix broken things. It helps the world spin 'round.

The world is large. And, yes, there are far too many of us. And sometimes we need to focus on our own insignificance. In the end, that's all we have.

I exist solely for your amusement.

I prefer a friendly interest in people and things.

We need to remember that the human race is made up of individuals, and each of us can make a difference in each other's lives. It's that easy. We can fuck things up for each other or we can make things better for each other. Or else we can do nothing at all. But, see, we touch people every day in metaphysical and physical ways. And, sometimes—if we're lucky—in sexual ways. And, sometimes, if we're really, really lucky, we don't get caught.

Plenty of people sleep with other people they don't really like very much just so they don't have to sleep alone.

There is a desire to be heard, to connect, to receive. But when the influx is so grand that it becomes overwhelming, we start reaching for the controls, and often blindly.

Any time I find myself being observed by a lot of people, there is a building pressure that makes me want to cut and run.

Whether or not we're seeking fame is certainly debatable.

I would, however, offer that what we are seeking is an audience.

Or, at least, someone to lend a sympathetic — or not so sympathetic? — ear.

Or else we wouldn't be here, right?

I like to engage in the world and I like to be paid attention to.

You've got to go where the audience is.

do I want fame?
maybe not
power and control?
call it what you want
I want it
we all do

I'm not going to be happy until every human being on the planet has read something I've written.

I guess I'm never going to be happy.

You know how sometimes you worry that no one will ever know how you feel? That no one will ever know what the point is?

I like money. I say go with money. And then write about what you did with all the money later.

Gain fame through artistic means and you can be as eccentric as you want. Without the success you're just another creep.

To all my ugly brothers and sisters: Whatever else we seek in this life, fine. But let us all work toward one unifying goal— to create a place where we can all eventually get beautiful together.

I don't know what you mean or what you're trying to imply.

In my humble opinion, I may be stupid, but not all that stupid in comparison with just about everybody else.

I often wish that I was so stupid that I was just happy and not concerned with whether or not I'm stupid.

The smartest Americans know how much the smartest Americans do not know.

Even though you're the product of your mother having a romp with a well-endowed, mentally retarded man, at least you're smarter than I am.

As a general rule, I do not mind earthiness. Except for those 50-something self-righteous hippies. Who do not have a sense of humor. That's fucking oppressive.

Today I gave a man in a wheelchair selling *Streetwise* a few bucks. A few hours later I saw the same guy walking around the neighborhood, shooting the shit with some friends. I felt pissed, and hoped he would see me and acknowledge the anger and disappointment in my eyes, but he was too busy having a good time.

Watching a couple of bums brawling in the street, both of them too weak and stoned to land any real punches on each other. That really gives you some perspective.

Beauty is symmetry. I'm not symmetrical yet, but I am working on it.

The truth is perfectly fucked up.

It's good luck to be shit on by a bird.

Silver birches release a poison into the soil, preventing other plants from growing too close.

I come across a dead bird fetus twice, three times a month. Honest to God. I keep a record of them in a journal.

Does that qualify as bird watching?

I've never once seen a dead bird fetus. That you see one on a monthly basis is simply magical to me.

I believe in coincidence. And I believe that's not necessarily all there is to it.

Well, there's coincidence, and then there's Coincidence.

Actually, no. There's coincidence and there's no other kind of coincidence. If there were a different kind they'd call it something else. So. Just saying.

A remarkable concurrence of circumstances or events without any apparent causal relationship.

The presence of ionizing particles in two or more detectors simultaneously.

'The occurrence of radioactive nuclide disintegrations within a time span too short for resolution by a radiation counter.

Abeyance. Conveyance. Purveyance. Creance. Ambience. Irradiance. Radiance. Expedience. Obedience.

Audience.

Although I might at times consider how fortuitous, strange, or merely humdrum in nature certain events in my life are—and wonder whether or not something was supposed to happen—I'm far more partial to the idea of actual coincidence.

Meh. I think we invent superstition in our longing for something spiritual, something transcendent.

If my life could be summed up in terms of groundskeeping, I would be a rake in a shed.

Something I read on a chopsticks wrapper the other day: "Chopsticks — the traditional and typical of Chinese glorious history and cultural."

There is no meaning in life. Only moments.

Wanting to do is more satisfying than actually doing.

I often go days without leaving my house because I am scared of people hurting my feelings.

Then there's the fear of living so long that I would become unable to accept or relate to the fear of living.

If identity is composed of the memory of the sum of our experiences, then surely broadening the limits of experience is enhancing our being.

The world has progressed so far beyond your frame of reference that you have become lost, out of touch, unable to focus.

There will always be elements that take you by surprise. And isn't it strange how hard you try to limit these instances, to try and act like nothing's ever shocking?

If we can't live with it, then the only alternative is suicide.

I would offer to help you but I've got a hole in the wall to stare at.

It's like my mother used to say, "God cares more about you being good than being happy."

Time is making desperate fools of us all.

Please disregard the advice I've given above.

Goddamn it, everything is so overrated.

My life falls somewhere between women and boredom.

Boredom may be the most Midwestern thing of all. Boredom is so intense in a place like, say, Indiana that you have to find ways to entertain yourself.

Boredom is one hell of a slippery slope.

Not sure if you were aware of this, but tortillas were invented in Kansas.

Spain is where the first black velvet painting of Elvis Presley originated.

I've often thought of all the work I could accomplish if I didn't have to work everyday.

If I had eternal life I wouldn't bother reading anything.

I get my haircut every three weeks. I like it a lot. I like the barber-shop. I like the process. I don't know what it is. Haircuts relax me. I like going in, sitting down, waiting, reading magazines. Some-times I bring my dog. We sit there together. I'm like an old man already. I have my rituals.

If you had eternal life, would you get your hair cut at all?

You're falling, watching the ground rushing toward you, hoping that before you hit the bottom you can pull yourself out of the nosedive.

My whole life: a lullaby, backward.

Sometimes it is not what we do that defines us but what we do not do.

I am a tattoo on the chest of a tattoo artist tattooing a tattoo of a tattoo artist tattooing a tattoo on my chest.

It's nice to see you're alive. I've been wondering about you.

How I do really exist.

I recognized myself in your nervous laugh.

Wouldn't the world be a better place if we all spoke a universal language?

What is my destiny? Will I be rich and famous? Will I stay hungry? Will I find my piece of the American dream — the beautiful wife, a couple kids, a sprawling house with the wraparound white picket fence? Will I die young? Will I live forever? Will any of these questions be answered?

Anyone who thinks God is interested in answering questions, look no further than the last chapters of Job.

America is known for its technology. We have giant telescopes that pull in the stars. We have kick-ass mega-quick computers and sleek phones that take color pictures. We have fast cars and razor-thin TV sets. So why in the hell can't we make a silent vibrator?

I don't know. The sound is part of it. That's what makes a vibrator a vibrator. It's like music. I think they should be louder. The louder the better.

If you ask a question and the answer seems ominous, there is obviously something wrong with your question.

All the pain that comes from just getting up in the morning.

You will be penniless and living inside a cardboard box over a subway grate. You will have to keep people from smoking around my oxygen mask, and you will have to empty and clean my colostomy bag.

I'm of the opinion that no matter where you go, if you aren't with the right people, your experience will be less than satisfactory.

Trouble is, most folks don't want you to succeed.

Your constitution is a growing concern.

That's what you get for lying.

I'm not here to lecture you about wars or deforestation or addictive drugs. Nothing like that. I'm here because I have some questions I need answered.

He who stands on tiptoes doesn't stand firm.

The human condition has been beautifully illustrated by this gross illogic.

What a bunch of bores.

while the world around us slept

Growing up in rural North Carolina, I was always captivated by the smell of the air just before a rainstorm. The air was so fresh, so electric, so alive. Your vagina reminds me exactly of that, the North Carolina air before it rains.

And when it rains in North Carolina, it pours.

This just happened: I'm sitting at the library. I feel a gentle tap on my shoulder. I turn around and see a boy—five years old?—offering me an open book. "Look," he says, pointing to the title printed in large blue letters. "It's a book on pussy willows. See? *Pussy.*" The boy drops the book and darts off before I can say anything.

You say *vagina*. I say *bagina*.

Vaginas, vaginal fluid, vaginas dripping vaginal fluids. What more could anyone ask for?

I once had an annual exam during which, in the midst of some awkward small talk, the examiner's eyes suddenly lit up and she said to me, "Want to see your cervix?" Using a series of mirrors creatively, she succeeded in letting me meet my cervix for the very first time.

I sometimes wonder if American women are the only ones concerned with touching themselves and smelling summer-morning fresh.

Seems to me that the average white male probably spends about a third of his life sleeping, a third at work, and a third wondering if he's racist. Or sexist. Or both.

Where I live I always see pickup trucks with those plastic ball sacks hanging from the rear hitch.

> If you hung a huge menstruating vulva from the back hitch of your truck, they would be banned in no time flat. I get it, how hanging plastic testicles from the rear hitch suggests a sense of vehicular masculinity. However, outside of that conceptual context, plastic testicles hanging from the back of a pickup truck is obscene and offensive. Especially when in the plain view of children.

>> The pathologizing of menstruation and the all-around fear of resultant contamination is—historically speaking—the rule, not the exception.

American reasons for avoiding "uncleanliness" are likely not quite the same as those of, for example, the ancient Hawaiians. But the overall notion is not all that new.

When you don't have testicles you have more time to invent stuff.

You've tried to fight it for too long. But you need to let your guard down and embrace your testosterone destiny. Change your name and be done with it.

(Insert slovenly male American grunt here.)

I'm very much interested in all the vagina motifs in your work. But the bleeding is a slight (well, maybe more than slight) turnoff.

Thank you for managing to work a vagina into this somewhere—even if it was only for a brief moment.

I just returned from a tryst in South Africa, where I was shocked to learn of bullet-shaped suppository-like tampons. They come in unscented wrappers. Real hardcore stuff. I've never seen anything like them in my local grocery store. They did fit so nicely into my pocket. And if you string them together they make a pretty daisy chain for the top of your head.

Dutch slang has a useful noun, *de befborstel*, to refer to the mustache specifically as a tool for stimulating the clitoris; probably from *beffen*, "to stimulate the clitoris with the tongue."

You know, I had something to say, but all I can think about is this Google image of herpes I just looked up.

Please cut my balls off, Mommy. Please.

One never considers the possibility of a death that includes penile mutilation.

I was one day before 13 years old when I lost my virginity.

The highway lines, like shooting stars. The radio static, like talking stars. The countdown, the popping of ears, and God, deep in space. Oh, how You bring us down from free-floating in outer space, rapidly, back to the bucket seats, far too woozy to drive all the way home.

In the back of her pickup, she clicked off the television set and asked her companion to go for a walk. The two walked slowly, slapping at mosquitoes, taking in the cool night air, the smell of wet dirt, the surround-sound chirping of crickets in every direction. I felt a tingling at the bottom of my spine (when's the last time you felt *that?*) as I imagined all the things they would do together out there, while the world around us slept. Then they made their way back to her truck and spread out a thin layer of blankets in the truck bed and laid together, waiting for meteors. I watched and listened from the dark, envious, trying to control my breathing, head heavy with self-loathing, wishing I had what they had.

I have two things in common with crickets. I love to rub my legs together to make music and I love to fuck in the rain.

My ex-girlfriend used to rent an apartment on a lake, and whenever we'd get tired of being cooped up in her tiny apartment, we'd go out and sit on a dock and just talk and stare into the water. I don't miss her or us all that much. But I do miss being able to sit beside a lake with someone and just stare at the horizon in silence.

"You spend so much time looking for patterns," an ex of mine once said.

Stumbled in. Got sucked in. Stumbling out again.

My ex-boyfriend currently lives in the Bahamas. He spends most of his days swimming in the ocean. He shits in the sea daily. He told me something about it being okay because of the gravitational pull and the tide or something like that. I don't know. Sounds like bullshit to me.

I think you too should try it sometime. You really need to expand your shitting horizons.

Godspeed you, dearest shitter.

My ex-fiancée and I ate in a Paris restaurant last Halloween—she, dressed as a sexy witch, and me, as someone who had just gotten out of bed. Pajamas, toothbrush in chest pocket, severe bed-head. We got no acknowledgment from anyone. It didn't register.

Every time I walk the streets of Paris I get this strange, melancholic feeling. I can't say I understand exactly where it comes from, or why it happens. But when I read what you wrote, it suddenly became clear.

I lost my virginity at 21. Or maybe it was 22. Honestly, I've done my best to forget.

An evangelical jazz drummer asked me to marry him twice. Only to break off each engagement. Each time he told me God had instructed him to do it. God, he said, spoke audibly to him from the bank of a lake in southern Texas.

A molecular scientist told me the morning after our first night together that, while I looked "just fine," my BMI still indicated that I was technically obese.

I got married at The Church of Spilled Blood.

I once dated a chef who claimed he would only have outercourse.

Our relationship didn't get beyond the apartment-shopping phase.

I left my virginity in the 20th century.

> There were chocolate sprinkles and edible glitter in every
> hole. Sure hard to be in a foul mood after that.

A lawyer once broke up with me by telling me that while I was
comfortable to be around, and made every day an adventure, I
wasn't "thunderbolts and lightning."

I'm sitting with my fifth-grade class in our school's presentation
area. We're waiting for the *Challenger* to launch. And right at this
time in my life I'd finally gotten up the nerve to ask this girl, Julie,
to "go" with me (she had accepted my offer the day before, during
recess, so I was flying pretty high right about then). And then, of
course, the *Challenger* lifts off, and we're all sitting there watching
it rise with bated breath, *oohing* and *aahing*, watching it fly. And
then all of a sudden, out of nowhere, a minute into it or whatever,
there's the big horrific explosion and the confused silence and this
giant fiery ball and a long trail of smoke, and the announcers on
television are stammering through their horror and disbelief, and
the teachers are in shock, standing there with hands over their

mouths, trying to figure out what to do. I look over and see that Mrs. Hotchkiss is crying, snotting, fogging up her lenses, and the other teachers appear ashen and defeated, heads hung, hugging one another. And then they turn the television off and start the reparation effort, talking to us, trying to soothe us and make sure our little hearts and minds aren't shattered. And somewhere in the middle of it all, this girl named Marianne sidles up next to me—this is Julie's best friend—and she hands me a tightly folded note. I quietly open it up, and it's a message from Julie. It reads, "Hey … you're dumped."

> I hope the *Challenger*-explosion-shaped frozen crystals in your icy heart finally melt with the love of the good woman you married.

I lost my virginity under a running shower. I focused my attention on the standing water and wondered what was clogging the drain.

> Friends have walked in on me standing naked in a bathtub. I tell them I'm only washing my feet, but they never believe me.

When it comes to sexual intercourse, the research shows that wanting is superior to having.

I love sex. I've always been a very sexual person. I'm not a religious person, so I don't have those bedroom hang-ups. In the bedroom, anything goes. You know what I mean?

I got my first dildo at 17.

When I was in Amsterdam I saw a gigantic dildo in a store window. It was disgusting. It was long and lined with veins and had a suction cup at the bottom. I wanted to throw up. I took a picture of it but the film somehow got damaged and didn't develop.

Dozens. Small ones. Long ones. All shapes and sizes. Some of them have grooves. Some of them are smooth. Some of them have dual functions. Some of them are anatomically exact. Others are of another world.

And when the day comes that you send your girl out to become a woman, give her some condoms and tell her she can't come back until she's fucked a boar.

Her womanhood would most certainly be confirmed if she could succeed in putting a condom on a boar's penis.

Everyone wants to fuck a freak. Especially an attractive freak whose emotional issues lead to insanely dirty sex on a daily basis.

I'm terrified of swimming in the ocean. And not because of *Jaws*. But for fear of being raped by a dolphin.

I once swam with a dolphin that kept poking at my crotch. I asked the trainer what the hell was going on. She said, "Oh, that's just Goofy. She wants to mate with you."

Boston in January in the Combat Zone. The prostitutes wear down jackets over scantily clad bodies, trying to stay warm and look sexy.

I've always found women dressed for cold weather undeniably sexy. It must be the desire to reveal what's underneath.

I'm only a little sexually active.

I'm still waiting.

I wish you and your girlfriend lots of luck and a little ESP.

Wherever you are, I hope you're happy. If you remember me at all, please forgive me for all the things I've done.

Love may be the one thing that makes you feel bad for blowing other people. Love is the greatest blowjob deterrent of all.

I must be an idiot. It never occurred to me that there were people on earth who couldn't get themselves off. I thought that was, like, universally doable by anyone and everyone.

I am but an innocent.

I don't own a vibrator for the same reason I never learned to roll a joint: that kind of accessibility could turn a harmless habit into an addiction. And I know me too well.

I lost my virginity in a room full of people. This was before viral videos.

Thank God.

Mythology has it that Narcissus rejected sex and all human contact in order to get lost in his own reflection. The lesson being that self-absorption can lead to the sacrificing of the most natural human needs.

I fantasize about a sex orgy happening out of the blue in my classroom.

When I lived up north, my neighbor across the hall would host weekly sex toy parties. Sort of like *Pampered Chef*, but with dildos and lubricants and the like. The party host would pass out catalogs and products and would escort each partygoer into the bedroom for private demonstrations.

I don't know what's worse, being juggled at or having balloon dicks made for you.

My bachelor party was at a strip club in rural Georgia. One stripper (who wore hearing aids in both ears) put me in her crosshairs and nestled into my lap for most of the night. We got to talking, and she expressed anxiety about money and revealed her suicidal tendencies. The tequila shots started rolling in, one shot leading to another. My best man got ripped to the tits. He pulled me aside and confessed his undying love for my fiancée. Admitted that she and he had fucked, then stumbled to the men's room, punched the automatic towel dispenser's face in, and passed out in a puddle of blood, piss, and vomit.

A few years ago, in Cleveland, I went to a strip club with some buddies of mine. I enjoyed a lap dance from one of the dancers, a tiny brunette with stunningly large fake boobies. A week later I was working out in my gym, and there she was, my tiny dancer, working on her abs with the determination of an Olympian. I walked past her and thought to say, "Hey, I've totally seen your vag," but I didn't. I left her alone. I'm a nice guy.

Showing one's vertical smile to the world should always be intentional.

American women are strange creatures. And very strange in what they won't touch, hide, or cover.

No one will ever be able to understand women.

My ex said he couldn't understand me. That was after he said sleeping with me was like sleeping with his sister. He also said he was "an open book," even though he was a closeted alcoholic.

It's a dangerous time for the male gender when I'm in the process of losing my monthly liter of blood. I have this hard-to-suppress urge to kick every man I see directly in the balls.

True feminism seeks parity. Meaning, the two people in a couple show mutual respect for each other and allow each other some freedom to pursue individual interests, whatever those may be.

I lost my virginity to a woman twice my age.

Once upon a time, I had a boyfriend who refused to buy me flowers on the grounds that he didn't want to express his love by killing anything on my behalf. I tried to be okay with that. But he had no problem feeding mice to his snake, so eventually I had to break up with him. It didn't seem fair that for the snake, one set of rules. For me, another.

> One of the first things I used to tell men I was dating was to never buy me flowers. I used to tell them, "Giving high-maintenance wilting vegetation as a gift sounds like something you do to a girl you *don't* like."

Hot dogs and flowers don't go together.

First you have to cut them just so, then you have to fill a vase just so, then you have to add the contents of the flower preservative just so, then you finally breathe deeply, take in their loveliness, and once you really get to like them, they wilt, become wretched, and fall to pieces all over the floor.

Men are so fucking annoying, aren't they?

Every unmarried man in the United States is an asshole.

Men are lucky bastards.

If they had to bleed out of their bums for one week each month, you know no such thing as a tampon would exist.

I don't see why it ever became so wrong for women to expose their breasts. I mean, breasts are made for breastfeeding. But because men are aroused by them, we have to cover them up. It just seems so unfair to me. Especially when I'm at a water park and I have to sit and watch one chub after another saunter by, man boobs fully exposed and two cup sizes bigger than my own.

A couple of years ago I was acquainted with a young man who not only had breasts but very feminine-looking breasts. I mean, it was exactly like looking at a woman's body with a man's head. My first thought — *how unfair.*

The image of a man nursing his child is considered odd but allowable. Yet the image of a woman doing the same is obscene.

> Breastfeeding is natural and babies have to eat. People need to get over it. I wish our society could stop sexually objectifying body parts that are merely performing the function they were biologically intended to perform.

>> It's a sexist double standard. If my nipples are illegal in public, then I shouldn't be subjected to the nipples of male strangers who take off their shirts in public. Moobs or no moobs.

A sign I saw outside a café today: *Please Do Not Masturbate on the Rats!*

I'm strangely relieved to hear that you've never dated Ron Jeremy. You—well, how do I put this?—dodged one hell of a bullet there. I just know too much about the man. Let's just say that when your idea of safe sex is slapping your junk repeatedly until the STDs go away, this is probably not somebody whom you want to know in the physical sense.

I figured that not swallowing was the final frontier of feminism.

Autoerotic asphyxiation: greed or stupidity?

I enjoy buying tampons for my girlfriend. Why should I give a fuck?

Sex sells. Balls sell. Pussies sell. Boobs sell. Legs sell. Cock sells. Sensuality sells. Masculinity sells.

Which came first, the billboard or the porn store? I'm guessing porn store.

I always wonder what porn stars say about work when they go home for Thanksgiving.

I'm not gonna prostitute myself anymore. Wish me luck.

Before my husband and I dated, we were just friends. I went to his apartment all the time, for parties and whatnot. I never learned the way home. I seemed to get lost every single time.

The Deep South, driving my old pickup, my college sweetheart with me. Sun fell, and we pulled over into some field and started going at it. (*Finally!*) Exhausted, we fell asleep, and, to our dismay, we awoke hungover and wearing hardly anything at all, parked in the middle of an Amish farm.

I met Brett on a plane from New Hampshire to Maryland. He wowed me with his impressive knowledge of the *Harry Potter* universe. I thought his perfectly broken-in Red Sox hat was cute.

I watched him hand the baggage handlers his guitar case, all stamped with travel stickers and bumper stickers, and remember in particular his long, graceful fingers.

Reminds me of a time when I was flying one-way to London. Ended up sitting next to some dorky-looking guy—glasses, pocket protector, all the stock descriptors. He ended up buying me some drinks. Nice guy. After a couple rounds, he told me he was into white magic. He then proceeded to show me all the stone daggers he kept in his pocket—daggers that he'd used at different rituals. The metal detectors never picked them up, he explained. "And the funny thing is," he said, fingering a dagger, "when we get to Heathrow, with the way I look, I'll be able to slip through customs without a problem. But you, looking like a hippy and all, will get stopped and searched." And you know what? That fucking cracker-ass warlock was absolutely right.

I sat next to a four-year-old girl named Emily on a plane for five hours today. Normally I despise talking to strangers on planes, especially children. But I felt the strange impulse to talk to her. I found my chance when she received her bag of Sun Chips. Her little hands couldn't open the bag, so I opened it for her. Emily chomped away and informed me that houses don't have feet or hands, only doors and windows. But sometimes, she clarified, they have back doors.

Mine was a military man on his way out the day I met him.

She shares everything with me. Even the sea.

It was you who couldn't let go. You who couldn't let go of something you never had in the first place.

I hope you've done well and stayed safe and made it to wherever you were heading.

I have never once been in love. Don't believe in it, whatever it means. Don't foresee it ever happening to me.

I should have given him my phone number while we waited for our bags to arrive. I should've told him to call me sometime.

Keep an eye out for me when you fly up north again. Maybe I'll see you at Christmas, with your well-traveled guitar and your curly black locks. Just the thought of it brings a nice rosy blush to my pale cheeks as I type.

In my case, at least, the best love is relatively unspectacular. Maybe I'm just an old married lady, but comfort has really proven a welcome respite for a heart that is prone to exactly the kind of panic attacks of which you speak.

No matter how many times we turned each other inside out, no matter how much love we shared, our lives ended up nothing more than wounds that would never heal.

The critical difference between chemistry and attraction: Chemistry is when both of you feel it; attraction is when only one of you does.

> This is the neatest way anyone has ever explained love. It really is that simple. I never thought I'd be able to say that.

> > If you really want to meet someone it doesn't matter what you look like or say. Just wear some pheromones and you're sure to score.

I must finally learn how to find beauty and how to find peace beyond those first addictive breaths of infatuation.

I have no answers. I'm too romantic, too emotional and melodramatic. I just want to get drunk on red wine and end up at male strip clubs for the rest of my life.

You're a good person. There should be more like you. In fact, you should get married and procreate as soon as possible.

Please don't get pregnant. Or engaged. I need you.

You follow a series of paths and end up somewhere, beside someone who has the same obsessions you do, and then you're sort of
obligated to marry them.

I haven't been unhappy very much in my life. I've been happy over
just about everything.

Patience. Perseverance. Emotional control. Hydration.

I think marriage is a sham. We're fed the idea as little girls and
expected to want it more than anything else. Men, on the other
hand, are expected to pursue their own goals and have achieve-
ments before they rush into something and throw away their
future.

But what can you really say? You're obviously a bitter
divorcée.

You'd think marriage in the US wouldn't have to be religious, but it's much harder than it should be to conduct
an irreligious marriage ceremony. When my husband
and I got married on a beach in Maui we requested a
nonreligious ceremony. The officiator instead recited a
"two-thousand-year-old poem," which we recognized
immediately as a Bible verse, thus reinforcing the
unavoidable.

Relationships stink. You go to eat somewhere and
you come back smelling like fry grease, moldy

carpet. Lava soap won't get rid of that stink. Then you've got the steering wheel all slathered in grease. And don't you love it when you walk out of a restaurant and you have to walk by rancid Dumpsters to get to your car? The sad sour smell of the homeless, too. Piss and dirt and booze. To top it off, there's my husband's post-dinner farts. That's the sickest smell. But that's when you know you're in for the long haul. I've smelled dead mice, birds, possums, chickens. Rancid meats of all kinds. A human corpse. That one, I saw on the side of the road. That smell sucked.

My wife hates the word *fart*. She prefers *toot*.

My wife gets weirded out over dogs with big dicks. Well, not necessarily weirded out, I guess, but grossed out. The whole red rocket thing has a tendency to leave her rattled. I'm thankful that our dog is only moderately well-hung.

love and beauty
chaos and pain
midnight popsicles
sudden bursts of rain
closets filled with lovely bones
lonely, not alone
answer me this—
what do you want?

While, sadly, not even the consent of the woman is required for conception to occur, it does seem to me that, in a pre-birth-control era, females who actually enjoyed sex would be more likely to leave a large number of descendants than females who didn't.

The female orgasm serves no purpose.

Enjoying sex has nothing to do with the ability to survive pregnancy and childbirth.

I tell people I don't remember how old I was when I lost mine. But I do.

I remember that night when we made my poor mother define *blowjob* and a bunch of other terms, and she did so rather matter-of-factly, sticking to the facts, even though she was blushing all over. She thought we should know and that we should see sex treated without shame or embarrassment.

I remember when my father first conducted the sex talk with me. I was around nine—pretty close to the time of my fire-setting spree. My dad was very, very uncomfortable. He tried equating sex with sticking a broomstick into a mouse hole. That one freaked me out so much I remember crying over it.

Dad stood his ground. No way was he donating his schlong for the transplant. Can't help but think of that poor Chinese man who'd had his cut off.

How would one ship the phalluses anyway? Air mail or ground? And would he have to send them shrink-wrapped and ice-packed in poster tubes?

Generally speaking, inserting anything into a penis seems pretty traumatic in my view. The penis is simply not engineered for such an act. It's engineered to be inserted, period. To flip the script is to defy the laws of nature. It is deeply, deeply wrong, not to mention nauseating, horrifying, and terribly painful.

Like a bloated catfish laying eggs inside your bladder.

A lot of eroticism hanging about up in the trees, down in the dirt.

I have been in complete and utter love with myself for precisely 30 years now.

It may sound strange, but, really, I lost my virginity to myself first.

I have trouble with *lay* and *lie.*

I'm in love with just about all the men I've never met before.

After reading this, all I can say is thank God I'm not an obese woman. And thank God I do not have irregular periods.

It's like, do you wait for your girlfriend to come first? It's not the easiest thing to do.

Enough with the sex talk, please.

As I was lying in bed I kept thinking about a conversation we had at dinner in which I told him that I'd never felt as happy as I did then. I told him I couldn't believe I was leaving for France without it being me running away from something. For the first time ever, I was really happy. I had great friends and a man I loved. I didn't hate my job because I didn't even have a job. I lived downtown with no bills and no car to worry about. And the sex was good, too. Really, life could not get much better than this. So I wrote about it over at The Nervous Breakdown.

Update: I have trouble with more than just *lay* and *lie*.

Weighing the possibility of abortion as a financial decision. Nobody mentions that. $500 seems like a lot. Pulling out seems a lot more practical.

> My unborn children support Obama. If they don't I'll be sending them back.

> Abortions for some, tiny American flags for all.

> Easier to wave a flag than be one, I suppose.

A few years ago the fat-girl clothing industry decided that fat women would be the ideal canvas for big patriotism. Everything in my size was red, white, and blue and had big stars and big stripes.

Life is full of surprises.

I think it will be quite a few years before we speak about sex again.

Before I moved to Spain I had a premonition that I would meet a woman named Alma ("soul" in Spanish) and fall hopelessly in love with her and life would be pink roses. I've never met anyone named Alma. I did meet several Albas, which made me raise an eyebrow, but I quickly discarded them as not being The One. If I ever do meet Alma, I may just faint. Until then I will probably continue to be cynical and believe that it was merely desperate hope and superstition that kept the possibility alive. I no longer even think it will be a Spanish woman, let alone someone with a specific name. Life is not preordained happy Hollywood endings. Life is chaos.

There's this office building here in Clearwater, Florida, one of those huge reflective glass boxes. On one side of the building, in a number of the glass window panels, several locals swear they can see the Virgin Mary. No shit. There are chairs on the lawn below the glass so the faithful can sit and stare at the pareidolia and pray.

board

A guy who used to work for me recently dropped out of law school and entered the priesthood. I'm serious when I say this. Please give me an answer to this question: Which line of work is more corrupt these days?

In my bouncer days, I once tossed a kid over a balcony. He fell three stories and landed facedown, flat as a pancake, then he peeled himself off the floor, got up, and ran away. It was the most depressing thing I'd ever seen. I'm not a religious man, but that fucking cunt must've had some pact with a higher power.

A friend of mine is a jeweler. One day he took a phone call from someone claiming to have found a man's ring on the sidewalk outside the shop. The stranger described the ring to my friend. My friend said, yes, a customer of his had called earlier in search of that exact ring. The stranger was silent. My buddy mentioned there was a reward for the ring's return. "Thank God for the kindness of people," replied the stranger at the other end of the line. And then he hung up, and my friend never heard from him again.

I used to have an old mutt named Stormy. She was of uncertain origins and sort of ugly and ragged and didn't know any tricks except love. I could never debate that dog's worth to me — she was no pure breed, no watchdog, not much to look at, couldn't fetch a stick. I guess, for me, Jesus and the Bible are sort of like Stormy.

All we have is the moment and all that is holy or unholy is what we do with the moment.

Kierkegaard, after investigating all the world's religions, finally chose Catholicism because it fit with his view that life—and the very fact that we are living it—is absurd. He thought Buddhism was the most logical and therefore not in line with the reality of life as he knew it.

Pascal's Wager: Since we can't know if there's a God or not, is it better or more sensible to live life according to what might happen if it turns out to be true? I've always struggled with this idea.

Since we can't know if there's a God or not, isn't it better to live life according to the Golden Rule, to live your life how you want to live it rather than the way some institutionalized ideology wants you to live it, and then, when you die, you find out that maybe there's nothing at all and you completely squandered the precious opportunity you had to mold your own life into what you thought it had the potential to be?

It seems like a safer bet to me.

Surely, when the moment comes when we pass through the ultimate threshold, it's doubtful we'll have much time to consider anything, much less Mr. Pascal's wager.

board

I believe there is no sense in talking about religion with strangers, let alone close acquaintances. No point at all and nothing to be gained by it.

all you
gladhanding
snake handlers
root down
and I will effuse you
with praise &
reciprocity for all

Jesus was a teacher whose bottom-line lesson was the importance of forgiveness and acceptance. So, why do so many use their religion as a tool for spreading hatred and rejection?

God is immaterial to me. But I do believe in good and evil.

Americans love the whole "sin on Saturday night, get down on your knees and repent on Sunday morning" thing.

I find that I don't care what people believe as long as they believe it with some conviction, and, most important, that they've questioned their faith at some point along the way.

I am a firm believer in separation of church and state. I used to live in Atlanta, and I was outraged one Sunday when the deacon at the church I went to gave a homily in opposition to gay unions. It was the only time in all my life that I saw hatred from a pulpit.

"Hypocrisy and hatred" are not the purpose of organized religion.

If Hell really is other people, evangelicals have certainly done their part.

Organized religion has also "bred" millions of good people who have committed countless acts of human kindness for one another throughout history.

The problem is that a lot of people like to put everyone who believes in God into this one big, unenlightened, creationist, fire-and-brimstone-spewing, terrorist-act-committing, altar-boy-buggering, black-and-white-only-seeing group. It's inaccurate and offensive.

I had to enter rehab for my drinking in 2001. I had just returned to Illinois from New York to take care of my ailing mother, who had been fighting cancer. I went into rehab (long before it was fashionable, mind you) and held on for the long haul. I was somewhat shocked to see how many of my fellow recoverees based their sobriety on their belief in God, which I had no feel for at all. I had to wonder — was I going to be a drunk forever because of this?

Alcoholics Anonymous allows you to use whatever Higher Power you need to recover. The crowd I had joined was using G-O-D, plain and simple, and it intimidated me, quite frankly, as intense religiousness always has.

> A man takes a drink. The drink takes a drink. The drink takes the man.

I was raised Catholic and was forced to be confirmed at 16. I didn't want to be confirmed and I didn't want to be Catholic and the day that the Bishop put his hand on my head and called me "Margaret" was the same day I said good-bye to organized religion.

> I, too, was raised Catholic. But a funny thing about the Catholic faith, they sure have an interesting way of beating the idea of a true, loving, and forgiving God right out of you. And so, I am a lapsed Catholic. Way lapsed. Venti-extra-shot-with-whipped-cream-and-chocolate-sprinkles lapsed.

>> I am also a recovering Catholic. I remember our priest would fall asleep during the readings. One of the altar boys would nudge him when it was his turn to read the gospel.

>>> I grew up Catholic and just recently began to rediscover some of my roots. The architecture, the respect for silence, the contemplation. I'm an eclectic. I want only the best parts.

>>> The Pope is an irrelevant figurehead.

Most of these stories seem to go something like this: "I was raised in the [insert religion here] faith; I left my church; and now read on while I belittle my ex-faith and basically anyone else who might dare to believe in God as well."

Ah, another Catholic basher. How original!

Try speaking about falling out of touch with the Catholic Church, with Christianity, with religion in general, without bile. Make your point calmly. Defend your decision however you like. Levy criticism where you see it necessary. No need to pass judgment on anyone else who, as I said, dares to adhere to a faith. Thank you. You don't know how much these comments mean to me.

Amen.

It seems you follow the teachings of Jesus more than you think.

It's the church that keeps people from Jesus. And the Jesus they've tried to sell is no Jesus at all.

Just stay away from Mean Jesus, and I think everything will be okay.

I believe in a Jesus who comforted the disturbed and disturbed the comfortable.

I don't think I'd want to meet Jesus. Sitting around with a bunch of really devout Christians makes me uncomfortable enough. I'm always worried I'll offend someone. Let alone the Son of God himself.

I wonder what Jesus would look like today.

Barry Gibb circa *Saturday Night Fever* is the closest to what Jesus might look like were he alive today.

Jesus is the fat lady. So, shine your shoes. In the end, that's all you really can do.

I was raised without Jesus. But I think he was probably nice.

I'm a Kool-Aid peddler, and absolutely deserving of a cult following.

If, after I die, the devil takes my penis and puts it in a jar and leaves it in, say, a suburban home in Schenectady, New York, I'm gonna be pissed.

Everything is spiritual. Chickens are spiritual. I pray for all the chickens.

Theoretically speaking, there must be a shitload of chickens in heaven.

There will be flies! Enormous numbers of flies flying around you in perpetuity!

Hail Mary, Mother of God, chase the chickens around the yard!

Heaven is right here in the way we are with each other in this moment.

But you've got to eliminate the ego first.

When a hardcore ideological structure collapses, it collapses fast.

I don't understand why God runs things the way He does, but I don't want His job. I'll meet you in His lily field though.

I want a complaint line for life, a complaint line in heaven if it exists.

The "I" you speak of is God, and I welcome you both.

When I rewrite the Bible, it's gonna go something like this: "Do unto others as you would have them do unto you." And that'll be the long version.

If you carry a bible around with you, you get the religious zealots noticing. They talk to you and sure as shit they'll bust you if you don't know the Good Book cover to cover.

I've been Jehova'ed many times, and I always feel awkward, thinking, *Okay, give me the* Watchtower *so I can turn around and recycle it.* I'm not brave enough to invite them in to request an explanation of their strange ways over, say, coffee and cheese blintzes.

I am a feminist and a Mormon. They're not mutually exclusive. The Church has provided my family following the death of my father with clothing, food, and other much needed services. Our ward is strong and compassionate. I don't know where we would be without them. Regardless of ideological differences, the Church practices the words of Jesus Christ daily in works and reflection. There cannot be a better testament than this.

I don't think I've ever met a feminist who remained in the church.

Why in the world was I created this way? Why am I the one who draws the short straw? Why, pray tell, do I have the worst luck? Can I not win at something just *once*?

Who the hell is the "I" I speak of?

Rudolph the Red-Nosed Reindeer: a nihilistic, atheistic existentialist who vacillated between suicidal angst and quavering intoxicated torpid blues warbling. And that was on his good days.

Hitler was a churchgoer.

to find the voice
of God
look to art
art like
this
beautiful just beautiful
breathing words.

I bet God uses your name in vain on a regular basis. I bet he alternates between yours and someone else's.

We're like ants, right? I mean, it's the species rather than the individual that matters here. I'm extrapolating from the fact that half a million women die each year in childbirth. So, if God designed the system, then those are God's odds on reproduction. Which means that this is an acceptable waste to God.

So, if we're the ants, does that make God the bored kid with the magnifying glass?

Does it bug you when people refer to "the universe" (i.e., "The universe knew I was sad and sent a baby squirrel to my window") when they actually mean "a god of sorts" but don't want to sound uncool in front of their friends?

Birds fly over the rainbow: Why can't I?

I only reveal my secrets to good little children—not bad girls who have marathon sex with epileptic boys in Pluto costumes.

Best of luck in your future endeavors.

This only makes me want to go skinny-dipping with the two of you either in the metaphorical, the real, or the biblical sense.

Imagine my grandmother's disappointment when I announced that I don't want to get married or have children. I'm saving the "I'm no longer religious" speech for later.

The good thing about God's loans is that they don't have any paperwork, the bank isn't involved, and God doesn't foreclose on you. The loan just expires.

I called God and asked Him your questions and He said thus: "Verily I say unto you my children: It's not about having the right answers, only the right questions."

Everyone should work a season or two in the kitchen of God.

All religions are as much reflections of man as they are of divinity.

Personally, I reject evangelical Christianity because I believe it's antihuman.

And to hell with the devil and his vast collection of Crocs!

There are lots of misconceptions about atheists floating around.

The chances of an atheist being elected to major political office are less than that of a Satanist. At least the latter shows hope of switching sides, whether or not those sides exist.

I must admit I'm a pretty stern atheist in the face of the Judeo-Christian monotheism of today. Yet I'm quite spiritual, agreeing and submitting to the idea that there is some sort of mass of energy that is much greater than I am. I don't think it can talk to me or me to it.

Figuring out that organized religion is a sham is merely the end of the first act.

Behind the curtain there is no wizard. Then again, I was born to carnies. I think everything is a work.

I'm pretty sure I was born with a prehensile tail, and my parents are afraid to tell me. I've got this little vampire-bite-looking thing above my coccyx, too.

Even if you don't believe anymore in what you have been taught, at least you have a point of reference to relate back to.

There are more than 50 mentions of the word "hell" in the Bible, and not a single one refers to a place designed to torture people.

I hope there's a place, somewhere, where we get back everything we lost. For good.

the Kingdom is now,
or so says the old rabbi

I'm looking forward to the confetti. And I'm pretty sure the Prince of Darkness will complain about the bubbles.

From the moment I met Albert I was convinced that I wanted to become Jewish. I went home and told my parents. My mother loved the idea. To this day, she still refers to herself as my Jewish mother. My dad, however, wasn't very excited. It didn't have anything to do with anti-Semitic beliefs or anything. He simply didn't want to spring for a bat mitzvah.

We are all Jews in the eyes of God, awaiting the Promised Land.

SHEMA YISRAEL ADONAI ELOHEINU ADONAI ECHAD.

Dad studies Buddhism and Zen philosophy. Mom gets her spiritual messages from passing birds of prey.

Farts smell the same when you are meditating.

Buddha laughs with Jesus. Usually, at me.

I have a deep affection for paganism. It's so pure and sensible. In many ways, I think Christianity was humanized by all its pagan loaners. When you pay attention to the reported acts and words of Jesus himself—not all the liturgical claptrap his disciples and the Church slapped on him—they have a definite pagan ring.

The Druids were also good at taking the basic principles of paganism and tarting them up with their equivalent liturgy. Priests are the same meddling mockingbirds regardless of their religion.

I could use a bit of false religion, I guess. Without its guidance, I almost never have the energy or desire to get all dolled up.

All that matters is this right here.

How does something come from nothing?

Do you send baby squirrels to people's windows or do you have other things to do?

How's it all gonna end, anyway?

No such thing as an ending.

I understand your worry and apprehension. I have been on this road before.

I can't help but chuckle at reincarnation. Who'd want to come back and do this whole thing again?

If I could ask God a question, I think it would be: What God do you believe in?

I believe you believe what you believe. Yet I believe what I believe, too.

All we can hope is that everyone knows deep inside that he or she is an equal, and worthy of equal respect.

God has an equal amount of love and respect for all of us, regardless of our race, our gender, or our occupation.

God sits in the heavens and laughs.

My greatest fear? That God is an artist and life is an abandoned, unfinished work.

Heaven is so many dots unconnected.

Solomon: "With much wisdom comes much sorrow."

What a beautiful adventure into the secret realms of holy men and their collective intrinsic wit.

May the lord be with you.

And within you.

And without you.

appendixes
the los paradise
cosmos diet brains
angeles snow
driving
france
the living
pets hitchhikers einstein
city sense of smell las
energy
bugs dead vegas
life nature
diet
coke poop
the human
evolution
body

some fool's careful dreams

The human body radiates most of its energy through the top of the head. The second most radiant area is one's hands.

That "we only use 10% of our brains" thing simply isn't true. We use 100% of our brains. Which is why trauma to any part of a brain usually results in major motor, mental, or social malfunction or death. But it's probably true that we're not conscious of at least 90% of what we use.

I read somewhere a few days ago that the appendix might actually have a function.

> When your appendix gets infected and has to be removed, usually it's because a piece of hard crap got stuck in the opening that leads into the appendix, and then you've gotta get your appendix removed before it bursts or things get messy.

> The function of your appendix is to cause you constant intermittent anxiety. Is it about to burst? Has it already burst? Has peritonitis taken over your gut? Is death imminent?

Men were more far-ranging in their travels, often venturing into unfamiliar territory (hunting, etc.), and women (often burdened with young hominids) tended to stay closer to home and visit the same spots regularly (foraging, etc.). As per the survival tasks required of each sex, the different navigational skills actually became a matter of evolutionary selection.

> Of course, the lines are not set in stone, and there are exceptions, but there is a statistically significant cross-cultural trend.

Evolution is natural. Some of us develop wings; others, blinders. Stagnation is for inanimate objects. Sometimes the pain of evolution is just too much.

The interior of an atom, adjusted to scale, is emptier than the solar system.

The most wished-upon star is actually a planet.

Sometimes I wonder if we're all just part of some cosmic equivalent of *The Sims* being played by one citizen of the Q Continuum with a particularly sick sense of humor.

> It sounds like you take the universe very personally.

> > What's the Q Continuum?

Just maybe, perchance, you are someone's world and universe.

I once had a roommate who claimed he saw a UFO. After college, he became a proctologist.

I did a science experiment in seventh grade. The effects of pollution on mice and plants. My choice of pollution? Cigarette smoke. I had the control mouse and the variable mouse. Same with two plants. I had a giant jar and I cut a hole in the lid and attached a tube and a funnel. My mom did the smoking part. The smoking plant got yellow spots. I performed an emergency intervention on the smoking mouse by rubbing his little chest so he could breathe fresh air. My mom made me document that I got too emotional and could not complete the experiment on the mice. I won a second-place ribbon.

I murder every single bug that crosses my path.

The best thing about ants is that they are mostly female. Only a few males are born to procreate and then they die.

What can replace the experience of a sunrise on a mountaintop, a still lake in the morning, a rare bird startled out of a tree just above you, or the simple clean smell of ocean air?

When I moved to the mountains I bought this awesome bed made of wood that looked log-cabin-like. It had all of the natural splits and crevices that are dark and damp—the perfect place for a spider to take up residence. We ignored our neighbors when they told us to make sure we had an exterminator on speed dial; I was ignorant and thought I didn't need one. A spider here, a bee there, ants like scavengers—that's what Raid is for. One morning I woke up with a swollen, throbbing arm. It hurt like hell. I could see two little red puncture wounds. The pain lasted for days, but I did nothing other than pop some Benadryl. Then my husband woke up one morning with the same wound on his left arm and the next day on his right. His pain was worse than mine and his skin was purplish. We finally called the pest control folks, who came out and discovered the brown recluse.

City life is all-encompassing for some people. People can be surrounded by city and never become curious about nature. They never think about how food is grown in soil, or how it gets there in the first place.

Exposure matters. If you've ever grown vegetables, you appreciate how difficult it can be. And consequently you are concerned about the future of food production. The same goes for the land and the trees and the mountains.

I was at the park last summer and this little boy was holding his littler sister's hand. He was five and she must've been about three.

Not far from the children stood a pretty young woman waiting patiently while her pug pooped in the grass. The kids watched, and watched some more. The woman knelt down to collect the pug poop in a designer shopping bag. "So, kids," she said. "Where's your mommy?" The little boy ignored her question and said, "Why are you taking his poo?"

I sometimes see people with Great Danes. These dogs crap like horses, dung piles the size of manhole covers. I always think to myself, *I'm so glad I don't have to pick that shit up.*

To this day I cannot pass trash without picking it up and carrying it to a garbage can.

It's always grossed me out that while cats do bury their crap under litter, some of it must remain on their paws. They go and walk all over everything—sinks, counters, tables, my bed. I know they're supposed to be exceptionally clean animals, but I'm still sort of freaked out.

Cat and cat owner have to have equal hatred for each other for things to work out.

My cat likes to meow loudly after he poops in the litter box. He'll sit outside the laundry room and howl until someone comes in and acknowledges his success.

I accidentally poisoned my cat last summer. The vet clinic put her on an IV overnight. There was no permanent liver damage. It was horrifying. She's been kind of "off" ever since. Doesn't come inside much anymore. Just lies under the shady tree in the backyard.

I wonder if my Bobaleena is still alive. God, I hope so. She was the best cat I've ever had, and a helluva lot better than this little miniature panther-demon I have now. This cat I have now likes to randomly attack me when I'm sleeping and watches me go to the bathroom. Maybe my negligence in leaving Bobaleena with an irresponsible woman is the reason I now have such a bastard black male cat. He's the opposite of my Bobaleena in every way: pitch black, unaffectionate, aggressive, whiny, and unpleasant to my visitors. I still blame my ex for insisting she would "take care" of Boba while I was living in San Diego, trying to figure out a way to move her West. It was a bad idea. My ex basically left her with the other college kids who lived in the house she moved out of. I don't blame you for running away, Bobaleena. I would've done the same thing.

My miniature dachshund has figured out how to use triangulation with mirrors. So she can look at me without straining her neck.

My dog is a terrorist. He runs maniacally around the house, growling at himself, pooping in corners, chasing his own tail.

Question 1: How do you fit 100 puppies in a bathtub? (Answer: Food processor.) Follow-up question: How do you get them out? (Answer: Nacho chips.)

Try this recipe for an awesome blended beverage. You will not be disappointed. Put approximately four cups of ice-cold water in a blender. Add one Shih Tzu, a tablespoon of soy protein powder, two tablespoons of nonfat powdered milk, six ice cubes, and four tablespoons of orange-flavored generic Metamucil. Blend until ice is crushed. Bon appétit.

I eat oranges. I drink orange juice. My piss is basically orange juice. I should be sick to death of oranges, but as far as I can tell they actually work. My teeth are hanging in there just fine. My eyes are bright. My skin is turning orange, as is my hair. I've got mild diarrhea. People look at me like I'm a circus freak.

I sprinkle Flintstones vitamins on my salads. Is that weird?

In America, we're always eating on the run. We eat in our cars, at our desks at work, on the couch. Places where it's difficult (if not impossible) to use utensils. Even when we eat at a restaurant we feel the pressure to finish our meals quickly, so we can leave and make room for the next customer.

Beaks on my knees. That's what I'm waiting for science to deliver.

I bite my fingernails. Which is why I have none.

I couldn't imagine living in a volcano. Though I wish I had the chance. I did camp at the base of Mt. Shasta once and got drunk and almost bawled because I realized that the mountain had the power to make terrifying changes.

> I think volcanoes are glorious. I love them. But night terrors? They ruin us all.

One day, if we are lucky, we will all finally step out of the too-tight underwear of time.

What happens to me if I stand directly on a time zone line?

I think they should freeze us in liquid nitrogen and shatter us like glass roses when we die.

The space program isn't doing so well right now. Isn't it weird that my car is newer than the space shuttle? My car also has more computing power than an Apollo spacecraft, and yet we're currently having trouble even getting people off the ground.

Consider, if you will, the amount of energy it takes to transport organic produce from the farm to your local grocery.

I can no more consider "energy" than I can God.

The planet thanks you anyway.

Oh, to watch Einstein lick an ice cream cone. I'd give my left arm to see that.

Something about Einstein's eyes in a jar makes me want to go rescue them.

I'm inhaling oxygen particles that she exhaled mere moments ago.

I feel like a scientific experiment gone horribly wrong.

A computer nerd. A comedian. An actor. A freak of nature. Ruler of the world.

A brothel keeper. A wise-ass pimp. Swindler. Black-market operator. Go-between. Fixer.

The poor lemming has been maligned again: The lemming, in truth, does not run toward the edge of a cliff following the pack. This is an unfounded bad rap.

Scientists say that sense of smell is most closely linked to memory. That seems logical. When I smell freshly cut grass, I'm taken right back to my Arkansas childhood and all those summers spent mowing the lawn.

When I smell freshly baked donuts, I'm taken back to that bakery job I had when I was 16 and how I'd sometimes have to pry bumblebees loose from the freshly glazed donuts.

And when I smell burning hair and shit, well, I think of very bad people.

I want to go to a dance club that smells like fresh cut trees.

I happened to know you in a parallel universe. I ran a rickshaw for you for a few months. You seemed like a really cool cat to work for, but in the end you turned out to be a real tight-ass loudmouth son of a bitch.

Car wrecks can be fun so long as nobody gets hurt. You just have to coordinate them well, make sure the other person has insurance and all that.

The house I grew up in Bay Ridge, Brooklyn, had a massive Cedar of Lebanon in the teeny front yard. When the horrible people who bought the house moved in, the first thing they did was cut down this enormous tree—twice the height of the two-story house! I actually cried when I revisited the house not too long ago. How could they not see the same beauty as I?

Incomprehensible.

I have never before heard of a male hummingbird doing a court-ship display without a female being present. Can anyone offer an explanation for this?

The snow that falls outside my window, the perfectly formed del-icateness of it, a gift of nature — quick, impermanent, complex. Like your dead friend.

Living on Pluto has its pros and cons, I guess.

Unlike living in Los Angeles.

It gets hot. Your skin breaks out in a heat rash. The streets stink because they haven't been rained on in months. You get colds because on errand day you run in and out of air-conditioned stores from the heat.

I would never suggest moving to Southern California.

I wouldn't mind, I'm currently marooned in Ohio.

LA would be great if you just got rid of LA.

When my parents were around 50 years old, they bought a cabin in the woods, in an area called Paradise. My mother lived there full-time; my father came up on the weekends. I really loved it there. I was completely happy. I loved living in Paradise.

I'd rather be anywhere in Europe. People there are slightly more relaxed over their meals. They take the time to savor their food, to sip the wine, to relish in a wandering conversation. Europeans chew their food completely before swallowing it. Then again, using a fork and knife does slow down a meal significantly.

Living in France was very hard at first because I couldn't work, couldn't find a place that felt right, didn't know anybody. But my memories of France are very, very vivid and I grew to love it.

Yep. Southern California's on fire. Air tastes burnt. Smokey. Apocalypse. Good run. It's over now.

There are many, many things that are true of the nation as a whole, that are not true of California. And vice versa.

> If you ever get sick of winter, you should move to Los Angeles. It's springtime all year-round. But of course the sky is brown, which is kind of a bummer.

>> I hope I don't meet any celebrities on my vacation. I don't want any distractions.

Number one thing I don't miss about living in America: driving.

> Someone has just finished yoga and is driving her suv to Whole Foods for sesame kale and a bottle of organic wine.

Nothing interesting happens anywhere. Unless you pick up a hitchhiker.

I once saw Walt Whitman standing on the side of the road in Florida, hitchhiking.

The buffalo stuck his head right in the car. His head was so big. And his tongue. Good God.

Every labored step a labor of love, every labored breath a breath of life.

I'm really glad I didn't have to resort to burning my car in a nearby field or crashing it on the highway. That could have turned out pretty badly.

I love when I read something and it makes me want to set things on fire for no other reason than to watch them burn.

I have an intense desire to take these two rosy-cheeked children standing in line with me and run them right through the deli's cheese slicer so they'll stop whining about not getting ice cream.

Everyone should break down at least once in the sad mad starry desert.

Nevada is followed either by Utah or Arizona, sometimes both, but never neither. All going by, in a spectacular blur.

Once upon a time I fell in love with the idea of living in exile in Las Vegas. I ended up living in Santa Fe instead, for six months, in a small adobe casita with a fenced courtyard a few blocks off the plaza. On the edge of safety with my stargazing dog.

I've never been to Vegas, and I just can't summon any enthusiasm for going. It seems like Vegas would trigger either profound depression or regret for me. But I like Vegas stories. I like reading about other people's depressions and regrets.

The beauty about New Mexico is that every town, village, intersection of two roads has a story, an echo of some fool's careful dream. I can't decide which story to tell next, but I promise it will be strange and uneven.

The thought of someone like you in Las Vegas comforts me.

Nietzsche foresaw the future, a newer strain of neurosyphillis that made the old look tame: *neurointernetitis*.

Sleep medication puts you in that wonderful half-awake, half-asleep state. Where you start talking about farm animals and toothpicks to the person beside you, and you're confused that they don't understand what you're saying.

I love that state.

Do you ever wonder if maybe America peaked in 1969?

An entire generation of peoples tethered to an instrument by what seems to be the tiniest of leashes, their brains engaged yet damaged, staring into flickering, poisoned screens, lethargic yet caffeinated, stirred yet indifferent, inactive yet infected and infecting, dead-eyed and desperate, wanting everything and nothing, gobbling information and hemorrhaging insight, legions of the living dead.

Here's to hoping there actually will be a year 2030.

war of the worlds

wayne gretzky

movies

wonder woman

football

everybody loves raymond

the american dream

television sports

g.g. allin

muhammad ali

deion sanders

moon

underdog

flavor of love

out of africa

celebrity

escape

dark side of the moon

kiss

diff'rent strokes

the clash

reality

tony bennett

robbie knievel

running

bigfoot

oprah winfrey

cleveland cavaliers

colonel sanders

the definition of wack

I used to be so entranced by the television that I wouldn't notice anything around me. Someone could have robbed the place and I wouldn't have known.

My mother was the same way. She would come home from work, make dinner, and then sit in front of the television set in the dark. I can recall having to say her name several times just to snap her out of her trance. This always disappointed and angered me, but I still have a television, and I probably act the same way when I'm watching a basketball game.

My dad used to come home from work at the post office, turn off all the lights in the living room, fall into his La-Z-Boy, and listen to *Dark Side of the Moon*. He would eventually pass out from exhaustion and a bit of the drink.

Nothing wrong with sitting around and drinking vodka.

It's the American dream.

Steer him away from cheap vodka. Hell, cheap liquor of any kind.

Bad habits come and go, people find their way. I don't need lyrics to tell me how I feel or how the opposite sex feels. Everyone has their own pain, men and women both.

When I was a young kid, I remember my dad explaining to me that *Wonder Woman* had to be cancelled because production "had reached the technological limit, in terms of wardrobe tightness." Looking back on it, it's kind of cool that my mom didn't seem the least bit threatened by my dad's appreciation for Lynda Carter and that costume of hers.

As a little girl, I watched the *Underdog* cartoon fervently, faithfully, *obsessively*. That funny music at the end still makes my eyes well up. And I never, ever noticed that Sweet Polly had a camel toe.

My mother wouldn't let me watch sitcoms when I was growing up. I remember her turning off *Diff'rent Strokes* right in the middle of the infamous Nancy Reagan episode, and then I remember crying.

There's this one episode of *Everybody Loves Raymond* that reminds me of myself as a kid. Ray's daughter is just sitting there on the couch, a far-off look in her eyes, and a big goofy smile. Raymond asks her what she's thinking about. She says, "Candy." I was once that little girl.

Oddly I think I'd have to credit American television for my desire to travel the world. I always wondered how the old folk in my small hometown could be content to just hang out in their own small community — there was so much more out there! But then, the time I spent in front of the TV they spent on the front porch. Both of us watching the world go by with a decidedly different focus.

People need to escape from reality. Doesn't matter what it is — music, video games, books, or movies.

I have the strange impulse to watch *War of the Worlds* now. The 1950s version. And eat a Moon Pie.

This is apropos of nothing, but I just turned on the TV and there was a Clash song on a car commercial.

Jesus H. Christ, the rules are swiftly changing.

I read this intense defense of television on Oprah's website the other day and I wanted to throw up. The author (I've forgotten the name) called television a "social unifier." That may sound fancy, but it's actually a pretty scary sentiment.

I don't own a TV because if I did I would watch reality shows like *Flavor of Love* or whatever and never get any writing done. I can't control my TV intake.

I get up between 5 and 6 AM, five or six days a week, put in maybe three hours, then a couple more slightly less focused hours of editing in the evening. I really have to stay disciplined to keep my focus, especially on a novel with forty-odd points of view over 12 decades — not to mention one with Colonel Sanders and Bigfoot in it.

Shooting televisions is so rock 'n' roll.

> I think every musician should be evaluated based on how many televisions they've destroyed.

Give us any chance, we'll take it. Give us any rule, we'll break it. We're gonna make our dreams come true.

I have an odd affinity for football. These allegiances are formed during childhood, I think. Every Sunday. It relaxes me.

> I'd enjoy professional football a lot more if I had a large supply of Vicodin to dip into.

>> The other day my boyfriend expressed interest in going out with a buddy of his and "watching the ballgame." This was the first time in a year of being together that I've heard anything about this desire. I got mad. I really don't think it's nice of him to have fooled me for a year into believing that he's not a sports guy. He was making me think I wouldn't have to listen to the sound of sports on the television, which is the worst sound in the world.

>> Do you really think Troy Aikman is gay?

Just the other day I was thinking about the Philly championship drought. There was nothing in particular that brought this on. It just popped into my head one afternoon as I was taking a walk. There I was, on the sidewalks of Paris, wondering when a Philly team would win a championship again.

French people seem to enjoy life more than Americans. This is, in part, because they have shorter work days and get extended vacations.

I find sports of pretty much any type to be the least interesting thing in the world.

> Every arena, every team, every cheerleader, every halftime entertainer, they're all basically the same, each with a different color scheme.

Howler monkeys in NASCAR leather jackets demanding that I repeat the alphabet backward while I shave my shoulders!

> I don't currently own a television, but I'd buy one just to see that.

Wayne Gretzky owns a small handful of the few records that are considered unbreakable. He's permanently number one, and for the most part unchallenged. That's one reason why I love sports, watching the careers of these one-in-a-million talents unfold. True, unparalleled greatness.

Muhammad Ali's hubris has always made me intensely uncomfortable. I never know how much is real and how much is a show. In that sense — the persona sense — he's unmatched. Though I'd suggest, thanks in no small part to our media-soaked culture, that Tyson is shaping up to be Ali's antithesis. The black hat. The legendary joke. I suppose we won't know until he's dead.

> This kind of situation boggles my mind, whether it's Ali or Gretzky or someone else. "That's it folks; you've seen the best. There won't be any more. But please, please, *please* keep watching."

Never trust a man who doesn't appreciate at least one sport.

buffalo sabres
have a buffalo mascot,
no sword. this is zen.

You miss 100% of the shots you never take.

My brother tried to get Deion Sanders's autograph once during the MC Hammer era. When Deion, who had recently appeared in one of Hammer's videos, refused to sign for him, my brother yelled after him, "I thought you were too legit to quit!"

My old roommate in LA had to get a restraining order against Robbie Kneivel. He kept hiding in our bushes, hoping to see her.

I know that has nothing to do with this but I felt the need to tell someone.

I met one of the Cleveland Cavaliers cheerleaders this year. Got her number at a nearby bar, and she told me to go to the next night's game and say that I was her boyfriend so that I could get front-row seats. I happened to have tickets and went, and she acted like she'd never seen me before. She totally ignored me. What's up with that?

The Olympics are a funny event. It's one of the few times people can be overly nationalistic without having to deal with any undercurrent of violence.

> We should remember that the Olympic torch relay was invented by Joseph Goebbels for the glorification of the Nazi regime and was not part of the classical games.

We have a roller derby team here in Birmingham called the Tragic City Rollers. The starting eight: Wheelie Nelson, Garrison Killer, Southern Discomfort, Punkin Disorderly, Purgin Mary, Dyke Tyson, Blue Skate Special, and George Squashingfun Carver.

I was running every day for a while to prepare for a police physical-fitness test, and it sucked for the most part. Even when I started making progress—and I got fairly decent at it—I still didn't particularly care for it.

We chafe, we blister, we puke. Then we sign up for the next race. We just have to keep going.

I don't run. I stand up. That takes a lot out of me.

I hike. I bike. I walk. I swim. But I don't run. I never run.

I get bored as hell when I run.

I don't really get the running thing either.

I suppose they're masochists to some extent.

Me, I'm not much of a runner. Only if I'm running for my life, which, truth be told, I've actually had to do a few times in the past.

It's really the feeling of running away from something that is most satisfying. This so rarely is addressed by runners. It's primal.

I once shit my pants while on a run. This was in college. I was right in the middle of a 15-miler and I just shit myself. It hit me quickly and violently. There was no time to react. There was no stopping it. My little running shorts started filling up, and were brimming with feces seconds later. It was a long, embarrassing walk back to the training room.

I had this same exact experience, but it happened at a Conway Twitty show.

Once we played a show at this crazy club with black lights and disco balls and novelty machines in the unisex bathroom. In the midst of our "Buttermilk Bisquits"/"Me So Horny"/"It Takes Two"/"Groove Is in the Heart" medley the crowd began to pelt us with cheap latex condoms and other matchbook goodies.

I somehow managed to pick up two girls after a show that I'd played at Raji's in Hollywood. I had on this velvet dress that was shredded to bits after 45 minutes of beating the drums, soaked with sweat, and I still managed to swagger up to the bar after the show, buy beers for myself and the girls, and then follow them back to their place.

When I'm 85, I wanna break out into musical numbers and fondle my own boobs in public whenever I feel like it.

Focus, Mom, focus.

In Cedars-Sinai with an IV in my arm, a needle in my other, drawing blood. I had a show that night at a club here in LA. I feared they wouldn't release me and I'd miss my show. So I ripped out the IV and the needle and figured out a way to stop the bleeding and took off. Made it to the club on time and did my show.

GG Allin played a six-minute show at a gas station. He beat his "fans" with his microphone and knocked out a photographer with his own camera. He took off his clothes and jumped through a set of French doors and fled the scene in a stolen white miniskirt. The crowd rioted, and the bouncers beat them with tube socks filled with batteries and rocks. Eventually, the bouncers unleashed PCP-fueled pit bulls on the restless crowd. GG hauled ass to a friend's apartment, snorted three bags of heroin, and died in his sleep. Earlier that evening, before the show, he said to me, "You don't get what you expect. You get what you deserve."

CRUSTY PUNKS ARE PROOF THAT HIPPIES FUCK DOGS.

When I saw Jim Morrison's grave it really just bummed me out. It was covered in graffiti and beer cans were strewn about. I mean, I understand that a certain element of his persona was all tied up in that sort of lifestyle. But, really, I would've liked to have seen a little more respect.

You only have to look at how many people do drugs to realize that escapism is one of our lowest common denominators.

I listen to different albums for the different drugs I do.

Nodding, nodding, the whole time.

The Greek word *pharmakeia*—from which we get the word *pharmacy*—also means "witchcraft."

Take a few tabs, eat some shrooms, and chill the fuck out. It'll be fun. Promise.

Eating shrooms and listening to Radiohead? Too obvious. Getting high and listening to Tony Bennett? Life-altering.

Ambien ranks right up there with watching *Out of Africa* on my to-do list.

I once got scurvy from mainlining speedballs with my friend Joe, a pirate. I was unaware that Joe had scurvy. But, really, I shouldn't have been all that surprised.

My dentist is a reformed hippie. He loads me up on the gas. The good stuff, too. He used to keep a Walkman in the room and would let you listen to one of two tapes, either *Disraeli Gears* or

Are You Experienced? The best part was after the drilling. He'd run the gas on low for a solid five minutes, then he'd flash-flood your headspace with oxygen. What a trip.

The drug addicts who live next door to me swear that they've outlived the universe.

"Radar Love" brings back memories of driving desperately from New Jersey to North Carolina at four in the morning, cranked out on coffee and cheap speed, trying to arrive in one piece.

try as I may to become the island
I succeed
in only being the peninsula
always some lagging piece of
land
tethering me
the clothes, dust
the man, dust
but there is a radio tower
on the hill
red lights twinkle in the dawn
& somewhere near midnight
the static goes clear

Bigfoot is a huge Thin Lizzy fan. Most bears I know are into the Grateful Dead. Particularly, Kodiaks. Pooh Bear, he's into New Jack Swing.

"Uptown Girl" is one of the most tragic songs I've ever heard.

The lyrics make me want to rip out my fingernails with a pair of needle-nose pliers.

The unofficial state song of New Jersey is "Born to Run." It suits our inherently criminal nature.

They should rename every Colorado high school "Rocky Mountain High."

Yesterday, I had lunch at the KISS coffeehouse.

I once danced on stage with Michael Stipe.

I walked in on Stevie Wonder shaking off before the urinal.

I once destroyed an Ozzy Osbourne album out of religious fervor.

A local youth pastor gave us hell for our music, so we recorded an Amy Grant song on my buddy's reel-to-reel, played it backward, and—I kid you not—we heard, *"Here's your pussy!"*

Steve Buscemi sat in the eighth row. He wore a baseball cap for most of the show, but took it off during the encores.

board

I was quite amazed to discover how much steamed white rice could be found in Black Sabbath's dressing room.

I was listening to Tiffany on my Walkman around the time of these events.

You have a voice like a canary. I'm making it my ringtone.

My musical abilities are limited to the triangle. If you ever need a backup triangle player, I'm game. I'm a virtuoso triangle player.

True jazz does not resolve. Neither does God.

Heaven is the place where nothing happens.

I remember that line. Who wrote that? David Byrne?

Well, he had a point but he was completely wrong.

A lot of dogs in my heaven. Buster Keaton films playing against the clouds 24/7. A power trio of John Bonham, Jim Morrison, and Jimi Hendrix taking requests.

I blame rap music anytime I hear about office killings. Marilyn Manson, too. But then again, I've never worked in an office. And I couldn't spot Marilyn Manson in a police lineup.

In an interview, rapper DMX was asked how he felt about the possibility of America finally having a black president. DMX responded with something along the lines of, "There's a black dude running for president?" The reporter quickly filled him in on all the details of the modern political landscape. To which DMX replied, in his trademark growl, "Wait ... there's a black dude running for president, and *his last name is Obama*?"

Many of us love African American music and literature while never examining the subconscious racism that growing up in America has saddled us with.

Deep down we're a lot more like Barry Manilow than we'd like to admit.

The definition of wack.

Believe it or not, there was a time when Rod Stewart was supremely rock 'n' roll. The real thing— singing for Jeff Beck and Faces—like Keith Richards. Until he wasn't.

If you liked The Dead, I hated them. If you liked Pearl Jam, I said they were gay. If you listened to death metal, I hated death metal. Deep down, I was a poseur just like everyone else.

Paul Bunyan is the King of Rock 'n' Roll.

I read an interview with Beyoncé the other day. In it, she was talking about her career and how she was planning on "transitioning into legendary."

I have days when I feel like a fucked-up Chia Pet.

If I climb up onto the roof of my house I can see Russia. No, wait—that's Disneyland.

Like a salmonella-stricken R.E.M. fed them through a wood chipper into a mud hole.

Nastier than Oprah Winfrey pleasuring herself with a car battery.

It does seem, though, that celebrity has become its own punishment, doesn't it?

Especially for people like Michael Jackson and Britney Spears, who became celebrities before they became adults. If they ever did at all.

Celebrities do attract attention to important causes. And that's why they do it. That's why people want them to do it. That's understandable. The flipside, of course, is that people will criticize you and say that all celebrities are vacuous. But it's understandable that celebrities would advocate. Celebrities (well, some) are artists. Usually, artists are a product of their environment. They're able to distill something from contemporary life and communicate it in a unique way. So it's understandable that they would want to be patriotic and stand up for what they believe in.

> Look at a guy like Sean Penn. He's an American. As an American, I think it's his right to speak out. And he does. He goes to Iraq. He goes to New Orleans after Hurricane Katrina. And for the most part, he understands the issues. He's not just an actor who's lending his name to a cause. He's substantive. But it's a double-edged sword. It can reach a broad audience but it can also seem indulgent and false.

Most people live in a world ten miles wide and one inch deep. Media glut will do that to you.

We're social animals and we look to others to help us make sense of the world. The media often move as a flock, collectively determining the storyline of the moment. They're under great pressure from corporate owners, nervous editors, and crushing timelines; sometimes it's easiest to revert to the safety of what the collective wisdom seems to be.

> Celebrities are at their best when kept in *US Weekly*. They make me nervous when they leave their magazine habitats.

I read that Lindsay Lohan got the word *breathe* tattooed on her inner wrist, in white ink.

Sometimes she forgets to breathe.

Celebrities are strangers. It seems weird to me to go up to a stranger and shake his hand or get his autograph.

Screw autographs. Autographs are for sissies.

Danny Glover resides in Cuba, crossing his fingers that his good buddy Castro will recover.

Kenny G on a moving walkway in an airport.

Tim Duncan eating ice cream on the Riverwalk.

Geraldo Rivera picking his nose in the men's room at the Nobu restaurant in New York City.

Spalding Gray riding a tandem bicycle down Stanyan.

John Oates in a Wild Oats.

Kevin Bacon smoking outside a French McDonald's.

Rob Schneider yawning at Stonehenge.

Bobby Brown putting cheese on a fishing line and throwing the line up in the air to catch bats, then placing the bat he caught inside a cardboard box and watching it through a hole he cut in the box.

John Daly power washing a Koi pond.

I'm obsessed with Tammy Faye Baker. Looking at her is like staring into the hole in a bowling ball. You think you can see inside, but it's actually pretty dark and you're not seeing anything but scratches on your own cornea.

Tammy Faye loved everyone: God, the gays, Ron Jeremy, even Satanists. I'm going to miss her.

I realize this will make me unpopular, but I like Ann Coulter. Not necessarily her opinions, but her strength. She's a woman in a largely male world of politics, and her opinions are unpopular with her gender. Yet, she's still strong and sharp. She's funny, too. I would go as far as to say that she's a good role model.

I don't agree with most of what she says, but I admire her strength. And I think all women should.

Rumor is, she uses a vibrator.

Ann Coulter is not an attractive woman. She's got a rat-like personality. This makes

her downright gruesome. But word on the
street is that the ones who are not so pleas-
ing to the eyes are the wildest in bed. In
Ann's case, I think this is definitely true.

Do you think Hillary Clinton is a vibrator girl or a dildo girl?

The pop culture obsessed: more proof of adulthood delayed.

Extended adolescence is a luxury of the economically privi-
leged. If you're poor, you're fighting some stupid war or
working your ass off in a kitchen by the time you're 18. If
you're not poor, you get to go to college and your parents can
worry about your alcohol consumption and promiscuity
because of some story the local news ran called "Hidden
Dangers of Your Kids and Spring Break."

Celebrity labia is the new cleavage.

A few years ago in New York I collided with Ethan Hawke, nearly
causing him to drop his baby. Uma Thurman, who had a surpris-
ing blush of acne, came trotting along after them. They were so
tall and thoroughbred-looking. Titans to us mere mortals.

June of 1989, I was in London, attending the premiere of
License to Kill, the latest James Bond flick. After the crowd of
onlookers had dispersed, I remained at the theater, convinced

that there were more stars to see. Sure enough, Patrick Swayze came out the side door. A mob formed, screaming. I got swept up in it and landed chest-to-chest with Swayze, only a policeman's arm separating us. I whispered, "I love you," and I like to think he heard me.

I used to be the guy in the costume. I was Goofy. It was like a drug, having people want to hug you all the time.

I once read inside of a Snapple cap: "Not every man in a mouse suit is a pedophile."

In person, Jewel is much more goofy looking.

I've seen Jewel around LA a bunch of times. She isn't goofy looking at all. In fact, she's drop-dead gorgeous.

Really? Did she get her snaggletooth fixed?

Had Jewel arrived on a camel to hand you an autographed copy of her poetry collection, would you be so bitter?

Between Jewel and Kirsten Dunst, I'm beginning to think something is massively wrong with the standards of celebrity beauty in this country.

My sister insists that all babies look like Elmer Fudd.

You sort of remind me of that character in *Little Miss Sunshine* who takes a vow of silence and writes everything on a pad of paper.

Whatever happened to the good old days of subliminal advertising? When Disney cartoons whispered, "Good children, take off your clothes." And the hiding of naked women in ice.

Alfred Hitchcock used to introduce a lot of his film characters by revealing close-up shots of their shoes first.

So you wrapped her in a sheet and dumped her out the bedroom window? Perfect. A coming-of-age movie set in a small town, with you as a boy in the lead. I think you officially have enough material for a screenplay.

I think you should have your own TV show where you're a crime profiler and you ride a magic unicorn.

You are the biggest fucking drama queen on planet earth.

Why hasn't someone made your life into a movie yet?

David Lynch helped me make sense of my life and some of the choices I've made. That probably doesn't say anything good about me as a person.

I've never understood David Lynch's work. His films bother me. I prefer to have things wrapped up nicely. I don't like wondering and never finding the answer.

Hollywood happy endings are what happen when you put an accountant in charge of creative decisions.

The bean counters aren't creative enough to actually create anything. If they were, they'd be writers and directors, not accountants. They stick to the formulaic to maximize the amount of money people spend who go to see their movie.

You've got to wonder: Why do accountants stick to this particular formula? The answer is that it puts asses into seats. People like it. People like to escape the hassles of the real world.

You may be overthinking it a little.

Personally speaking, I like a good film and mostly look forward to a happy ending. There are enough unhappy endings in my life as it is. I go to the movies to suspend reality for two hours, not to have more of it stuffed down my throat.

My favorite kind of ending is one that gives me a glimmer of hope. One that implies the possibility of future happiness through hard work and a minimum of fucked-up behaviors.

I want to be inspired, to learn a little more. If that happens, then maybe the film succeeds in having some sort of educational value, in addition to being entertainment.

I've grown tired of the Michael Moore approach to documentary filmmaking. You know, where the director injects himself right into the narrative of the film. I'm so tired of political polemics that preach to one side or another.

How about a film that shows us that the US is not red or blue, but a purple country, even in the most remote depths of rural Texas?

It behooves each party to demonize and stereotype the other—to draw divisive lines and oversimplify things into some lame dichotomy. There's this notion that small-town Red State America is packed tight with hapless hayseeds who are "other" and "lesser" than people in other parts of the country. This is simply not true.

Red State Americans demonstrate political viewpoints across the board, but—and this sounds trite—they are people, above all else. What I would say to Blue State America is that people in those flyover small towns are folks to engage, rather than write off. If the political parties and their rampant advertising—and the media and its lust for conflict—would get out of the way, I think we'd see

more connection and union in the country, which
would allow us, in turn, to face our problems together instead of across divisive lines of fire.

I would definitely like to see a film that reminds
me I actually have a voice in this country.

This is a pretty depressing time to be an
American. And I would feel that way if I
were living on the moon.

We got permission from the superintendent to set up the 40-foot-
wide mobile screen on the high school football field. It was a beautiful night and something like 450 people showed up, carrying
chairs, picnic blankets, and coolers. Most of the characters in the
film attended, which was somewhat surreal. There we were, sitting
on the football field where George W. Bush made his first public
appearance in Crawford, Texas, back in 2000, watching that exact
event appear in one scene. We'd hear the sound of the train in the
film and then we'd hear the real train go by a half mile behind us.
You'd watch someone have a transformational moment in the film
and then turn around and see them chomping on popcorn, gazing
up at the screen.

The plot: He's going to die; she'll live to tell the tale; the rising
action includes two chainsaws and a demonic printing press. The
resolution will involve plenty of sound and fury that eventually
amounts to nothing.

Girl meets boy. They like each other, and all is well until something terrible and seemingly insurmountable happens, more or less, at page 85 of the screenplay. Love triumphs over all and the movie ends with the kiss to end all kisses and our happy couple walks off into the proverbial sunset.

I bet the soundtrack will be pretty good.

But if the story sucks just as much as real life what is the point of paying $9.50?

It's pretty simple: Life is full of shitty endings, unhappy experiences, and things that turned out any way but the way we wanted.

Our parents are supposed to give us as many happy endings as they can.

Your childhood is the greatest fantasy of them all. A much bigger production than anything Michael Bay could muster.

Movies are fiction. They're fantasies. Made-up stories that give us hope — hope that keeps us from slitting our wrists or stepping in front of a bus. God bless Steven Spielberg for recognizing the lackluster lives of the multitudes and doling out hope to keep us in the game just one more day.

Something repulsive. Something to behold. Something for us to chomp popcorn, throw tomatoes, cheer, and boo.

Michael Bay needs to rot in hell.

Admit it. It's amazing what a blockbuster can pull out of a person. Even a Michael Bay blockbuster.

I'll admit that when the weekend rolls around, my liberal defenses are down.

In dark theaters we are all the same wherever we may be.

It's comforting to know that something so simple can bring us so much joy.

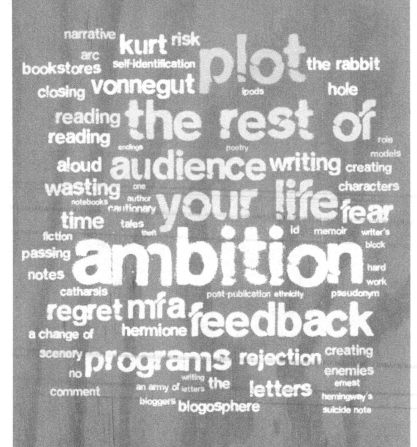

the depth of a corndog

The other week I was riding the L train and the girl sitting beside me was scribbling in a cute little notebook. I couldn't help but glance down and read what she was writing. People sucked. Life sucked. She sucked. A certain someone whom she had lost trust in, he sucked. School sucked. Work sucked. Her friends weren't really her friends anymore. And so on and so forth.

You should've reached for the emergency brake and jumped from the elevated tracks with her notebook clutched to your chest.

I have a couple of suitcases filled with notebooks. My mother recently passed the suitcases on to me to clear up some space.

I find myself hiding my composition book under my newspaper when I'm writing at a café. I don't want anyone to know that I'm writing.

Mine sit in my closet, taunting me.

The difference between a writer absorbing a public scene and a pervert doing the same is probably nil.

But, hey, if you've got a summer-long Eurail pass, and you just got an STD in Ibiza, fair enough. Write it down in your journal on a train, or in a quaint little café.

I write under the overpass.

I've noticed that writing near a body of water, whether it's a lake, the ocean, or whatever, seems to have a soothing effect on me.

I store my ideas, my stories, and my secrets in a piggy bank I keep tucked away safely under my bed.

What scares me the most is that when I come back to something I started a few days before, I usually don't like what I've written.

No matter what I type here, it's going to sound clichéd and full of arrogance. I know this because I just typed something. Read it. And deleted it.

I'm afraid of writing something I don't have the sense to know is terrible.

Is there anything one should not write about?

I have a hard time looking at my own handwriting. Sometimes it seems as if my father is the one controlling the pen.

Anne Lamott once wrote something about the writing process — the creating, the finishing — as being like tucking the octopus into bed. You can never get all the arms under the covers.

That's me — lost down that frightened corridor with the red walls and the green oil lamps, all the way at the end where you're not sure if it turns into something else or simply stops. That's me, on the right, at knee level, behind the brushed-steel duct, hoping that madness is reality. That's me, tap-tap-tapping away.

I've noticed a trend in my own writing, going from what might be called *absurdist realism* to something where the realism gets more plastic and bendy. I've heard this called *slipstream*, as well as the *New Weird*. But screw labels. All I can do is follow the rabbit hole.

W.H. Auden was obsessed with mining.

The basic premise is to create characters to which an audience can attach itself. To try and connect on a different level, not an explicitly intellectual level, and not on a political level, either.

Make a character want something. Everything follows from that.

My protagonists always end up being utterly convinced that they can easily do deals with others. That's not good. That doesn't say anything good about me.

Plot is hard. Plot is maddening.

Fuck plot. Plot is for best-selling paperbacks. You don't want to be a best-selling author, do you?

I don't need a plot. I want to live in your gray matter.

More stories about anything. As long as you are here, dear, that's fine with me.

Baby, sometimes your writing scares me.

There is nothing fundamentally wrong with the idea of writing as catharsis; it is the final step away from the reflection in the pond. You say it, you let it go, and, like a pebble in the pond, it sinks away, out of sight.

I am 60 years old, and the older I get, the more I fade. I am nearly invisible now. I am nearly inaudible. When I write, if someone reads it, there is a certain substance I gain. I am seen again; I am heard again.

Writing's writing and a writer writes what a writer writes.

Embracing the dangling modifier. Dotting your i's. emailing e.e. cummings. Polishing up the final draft. Clicking send. Chuckling the Bukowski. Trout fishing in your writing room. Bearing the lightness of being. Manufacturing consent.

I mean, really—what's wrong with being a writer?

A writer's life is a ruined life.

I feel bad for you. I really do. You've wasted a lot of precious time.

Someday, somebody out there will love me and appreciate me for what and who I am.

I don't want to peak only once. I want to peak a million times and I want everyone to clap for me.

I wish I could suddenly have lots of money from my writing.

It's completely fake, that notion of not being ambitious.

I'd rather be read than dead.

No fate worse than to die before the audience cheers.

Delmore Schwartz. He was this poet who published an amazing collection of poems, *Summer Knowledge*, when he was in his early twenties. After that, he never quite hit the mark again. Granted, he did some interesting things here and there. Taught at Columbia, had Lou Reed as one of his students. There's even a Velvet Underground song dedicated to Delmore Schwartz. But yeah, he never quite hit that high again.

Holy shit, I hope your books are only slightly longer than your bio.

I don't think you have to write 10,000 words to get 100 good ones.

I'm a huge fan of the underdog, the unspoken-for and the forgotten, and have little tolerance for pretentious prose.

The blogosphere, I think it's a huge net positive in human discourse. Not perfect, often very sloppy and self-indulgent, but better than the alternative.

This is a very righteous political time. Right-wing dogma. Left-wing filmmakers, trying to tip the scale. Not war, but wars. Scandals. Pissed-off Americans.

People are trying to pay attention, at least on some level.

The founding fathers had their own blogs. They were called *pamphleteers*.

This made me think about how, back when I was a kid, I used to put out this one-page handwritten newsletter complete with line drawings. It was about the animals who lived in the hills behind my house. I don't think anyone ever read it. I guess kids nowadays are starting blogs and websites.

Me, I feel frustrated being one of a million in this "army of bloggers" who are basically shouting silently as we type.

I think writing behind a pseudonym allows for a bit more candor.

Writers with strong personal voices are recognizable to those who know them, I think. Regardless of a pseudonym.

Honestly, I'm having a hard time typing *pseudonym* over and over.

I like your fake name. Although, I don't understand what or whom you're hiding from. I don't think you need to hide at all.

Only people who refuse to take responsibility for what they write use pseudonyms. Deep down you know you suck.

Esse quam videri— meaning: to be, rather than seem to be.

Passing notes was the best part of high school. Going into third period with a stack of notes, one from your girlfriend, one from your friend girl, from your best bud, from his girlfriend, from the girl who wants to be your girlfriend, and from your girlfriend's best friend wanting to know what the deal *wity'alls* been lately.

And maybe one from your ex.

Oh, man, I miss letters so bad.

In the past, when I used to do hallucinogens, I would scrawl what I thought were these amazing lines on my arm while I was in the throes of a trip. The only problem was that the next day I could never read what I'd written because either it was one huge mess or I'd sweated it off. So, yeah. I can totally relate.

Queen Victoria grew up on a farm in New England and took care of goats and chickens as a child. Then a bunch of stuff happened. Now Queen Victoria lives in New York City and writes historical fiction.

It was the early 1980s. Some Mexican thugs stabbed some black guy in the gym. A few days later, some black thugs stabbed a Mexican guy in the west block. What they thought was a Mexican was actually an Italian who had just completed a 15-straight sentence. He was sitting on the toilet when they hit him. He staggered to the cell door with his pants around his ankles, cradling his guts. He had only a few days left.

You seem free of writerly neurosis, which is both refreshing and troubling.

>I do pretty well for a guy who lives on fishcakes and cheap wine.

I got physically ill while reading this.

I will repeat this story as my own after a few cocktails.

I was reading Anne Lamott again, earlier this afternoon. She writes: "Everybody's just trying to find a place to be loved and not so scared all the time." I thought that was nice.

Where is the nudity? Somehow, somewhere, this needs nudity.

I'm imagining a sweeping, melodramatic, midlife-crisis memoir written by Sarah Palin. Written as a comic novel under the pseudonym "Sarah Plain."

"Unsheathing Fear: How to Identify and Corral the Fear at Your Center and Manipulate It for Your Most Genuine, Honest Poems"

You can't be a poet until you've broken a heart. Someone else's, or your own.

> The hell with poetry! Let's sit in the middle of the square and divine the life stories of passing folk according to the rhythms of their feet. Let's close our eyes and see if we can distinguish the waltz of a ghetto fly from the lurch of a day trader who just lost her shirt on a careless buy.
>
> There are no poets and there is no poetry—only poems.
>
> Shit, I can't read poems. They fuck with my eyes.

I was at a gym here in LA, on a treadmill. The woman next to me was reading *Waiting for Godot*. I thought that was kinda funny.

Reading something like that in a gym in LA. Where people appeared to be anxiously awaiting their own Godot—the next acting gig, a flatter tummy, a new girlfriend, boyfriend, et cetera. So I casually leaned over to her and told her how ironic it was to be reading *Waiting for Godot* in a gym. Needless to say, she was not amused. Not in the least.

Oh well.

Read in silence or read out loud?

I like to read out loud to myself in the bathtub. The acoustics are wonderful.

I do some of my best reading on the john.

Communal toilets in ancient Rome. Men sitting in a room, chatting languorously.

I learned about syphilis reading Frank Norris's *Vandover and the Brute*. Flossie—a hooker—gives Vandover syphilis. But of course he doesn't know it. By the end of the novel he's a madman, foaming at the mouth, howling at the moon.

I keep magazines in my car for the times I eat out alone. Reading makes me feel less conspicuous. I've done movies alone, but I don't like it unless it's a matinee.

I have four writing desks in my house. But the one I get the most work done at is the piece of plywood laid over two end tables, in a completely Spartan little room with only a bookshelf and a plant.

In the book I'm reading now, the protagonist describes a toast sandwich: a slice of toast between two slices of nontoasted bread, with ketchup or other condiments spread on its internal surfaces.

I read *War of the Worlds* last year and was surprised when I read a sentence that said something to the effect of "He ran behind her, ejaculating loudly." Obviously that word has taken on a whole new meaning in the 20th century.

I can't decide whether I want to read Michel Houellebecq or not. Seems as if the ideal location to read him is France and not Southern California.

> I read the whole thing while he cored out my chest and packed it with sawdust. I bought *Platform* when it first came out and it still sits in the bag. I have yet to be in the right place to read it.

I don't have the patience for fiction anymore. Or maybe I just think the real world is a helluva lot more fun.

Writers are in competition with iPods. How in the hell are we going to have a chance against an iPod?

I love it, but writing is such a limited form of creative expression. It's difficult to surprise today's reader, to really level them with the work. It requires total commitment on the reader's part. One page at a time. And the writer is burdened with unlearning all of the things he has learned.

I'm more interested in the traditional idea of the storyteller, sitting around the fire. That's how I treat it. I don't want to bore anybody. If they go away pissed off, I'm happy. If they go away happy, I'm happy.

I'm only interested in being the all-powerful Fidel Castro of my universe.

I remember picking up a James Frey book in a bookstore and reading a bit of it. I read the scene in which a priest tries to molest him in Paris and Frey beats him to death in the church. I closed the book right then and slipped it back onto the shelf, thinking, "Wow. This is absolute bullshit."

> I never understood all the hubbub about James Frey's work. Just move his "memoir" over to the book store's fiction section. Problem solved. Is that really so hard?

It bothers me that Hermione has to work so hard at being a skilled wizard. She seems more talented than Harry Potter and Ron and everyone else. Only, she's always outshined by Harry, who—by dumb luck—is born with skills he doesn't know how to use. Nor does he express the initiative to come into his wizardry full-scale.

When Harry is confronted by Voldemort, I'd rather see Hermione bust onto the scene, shouting in tongues, casting a series of sick spells that turn Voldemort into dried bird droppings. Saving Harry's ass while he sits there like an idiot, rubbing away at that scar on his forehead, distracted by thoughts of trying to commune with his dead parents.

Hermione should be class valedictorian already.

I believe that writers and artists tend to be, dare I say, a little more psychologically androgynous than the rest of mankind. The girls, a bit less girlie. The guys, a bit more sensitive.

My audience: hundreds of smart, good-looking young people fully engaged with words and books.

Reading aloud from my own novel in a bookstore is like masturbating in public.

I don't even go to literary readings anymore because they're so damned boring. It's the same thing over and over.

board

I once interviewed a Spanish writer named Lucía Extebarría here in Madrid. She hipped me to the fact that all writers are self-centered narcissists with extremely fragile egos.

Kurt Vonnegut, as much as I enjoyed a couple of his books, is probably an asshole.

> Vonnegut had his own problems with depression, alcohol abuse, and all the other flotsam of a wrecked life. What he communicated to me in his letters was a personal reaffirmation of overcoming these obstacles with a deep and mysterious love for life. The letters made me realize how close his life was to what he wrote. I believe that is why he was such a great writer, writing from the heart the way he did.

>> I must respectfully add that nobody draws an asshole quite like Kurt.

>>> I had Kurt Vonnegut as a teacher, briefly. I caught him at a terrible time in his life, just after one of his Pall Malls had burned down his New York brownstone. All of his writing archives, turned to ash. He almost died. He and his wife separated, and he came to live in Northampton and was writer-in-residence at Smith. I was working on my MFA at nearby UMass, Amherst. I took a class with him and it kind of broke my heart. He donned stained slacks and a filthy safety-orange sweater with holes in the elbows. He was drunk. He made inappropriate comments about the beauty of co-eds bending over to pick up

their books. It was clear that I'd caught him at a sad, sad juncture. I ended up dropping the course.

I wonder if the fire brought back memories of Dresden.

I have this theory that all of Kurt Vonnegut's books were exorcisms.

A genocidal, holocaustic, science fictiony, fantasy-like, futurist kind of thing.

I wrote to Kurt Vonnegut about my struggles with alcoholism and the AA program, and he responded with the most amazing letter I've ever read. He wrote about how he was in awe of the universe and how alcohol is the problem for every alcoholic, not lack of a specific religious belief. His letter saved my life. I had no one else telling me this. I mean, who would?

Kurt Vonnegut was like Spider-Man to me. He would swing down and save you, then swing off and disappear, leaving you to wonder: Who was that guy?

You know, Ginsberg and Kerouac spent a lot of time in Boulder. Word on the street is they used to run these outrageous parties over at the Hotel Boulderado, right off Pearl Street. Drank absinthe while braiding each other's hair and trying on each other's socks. A cluster of forsythia in a vase in the corner. Hundreds of angel-headed hippies skipped in and out of there to try and beat those two. Many tried, many failed.

> I met Ginsberg when I was 14. He grabbed my ass and asked me if I would go upstairs with him.

> > Beat poets, my ass.

Never trust a stable artist.

> Never stable trust with an artist.

> > I have no idea what that means.

I don't trust people who can't spend time on their own in a strange new place.

I've found that those who can step into a world so far from their own are the truly brave. The real ones, the ones who actually have the most to give.

> I've never left a hotel room without taking the pens.

> > My advice is to leave the pens right where they are and take the Bible instead. Then hide all the complimentary

toiletries in the ice bucket with a note that says, "You win! You found the toiletries!"

I love Sanibel Island. Sanibel Island is paradise. Sure, you'll probably end up wearing Tommy Bahama shirts and knowing all the words to Jimmy Buffett's oeuvre, but so what? You'll be happy, and once you're happy, depression and anxiety stop seeming like the only game in town.

Come to Nashville. We have nude bronzes, cowpunk goth girls with tattooed vultures descending on their Poonanza, the world's largest adult novelty store, and MTMHI, an asylum with an indoor swimming pool and a beauty shop. Plus, Porter Wagoner.

The fact that great places like these exist makes me want to build a stairway to the heavens out of microwaves.

Berlin is one of those towns I have a hard time believing actually exists.

I say a change of scenery stimulates art.

I've often thought the worse the weather, the better the art.

Fugue states are important to writers.

Maybe everywhere sucks.

I've lived lots of places, my friend, and I have to tell you: The problem isn't so much America as it is human beings.

They're everywhere, man.

Someone should tell J.D. Salinger to throw a potluck and smile once in a while.

The only literary agent I had died in a car wreck. Bless his ghost, I took that negative energy and spun a positive outlook, joined the media, and started networking in new ways. The book world, I have learned, can be penetrated from odd angles.

Aldous Huxley died the right way. That's the exact same way I'm going out, Jack—on a left-side trip down the rails of mania and psychotropicana!

And what was it Hemingway's suicide note said? Life is just one damn thing after the other.

These desperate attempts to convince ourselves that everything will be all right. When, in fact, things mostly are what they are.

Sad old world, get off of me.

A recurring theme in my writing, I must point out, and part of my novel-in-progress, is the swallowing of Drano. My neighbor tried to end her life this way when I was a kid. She didn't die from it. It's been haunting me ever since.

Just because something is true doesn't necessarily mean it can ever be written well.

You've got talent, but you need to lose the Kerouac hard-on.

Good writers find the proper balance between despair and hope. You, my friend, are only offering interminable hopelessness.

You need new role models. 20th century novelists and poets make for shitty role models.

Here's hoping that nobody ever refers to any of us as "literary Buffalo Springfields."

Jesus, the people you find on the Internet.

I'm constantly frightened that I've accidentally stolen something. Or that I wrote something and it was written before, but I didn't know about it, and no one believes me.

This happens to me especially with emails. I rewrite them in my head so many times that when I actually write them down I become convinced that I've done so already, and that the recipient is going to think I'm a kook when the second copy of the same message arrives.

That's happened before with certain subject matter quite a few times. I write about it, don't get it published, and then someone does it after I do it and manages to get it published. I hate my life.

Develop the narrative arc. Remember: rising action leads to the climax. Earn those clichés. Give your story a happy ending. Then submit the manuscript and forget about it forever.

Have you ever suspected that you've been stealing from yourself?

I have a terrible feeling that you're out there with writer's block because you can't think of a way to fit a vagina into your next story. I, for one, believe that your writing is probably still very funny even when there isn't a vagina in it, so I hope you won't let this be a hindrance to you.

Vagina or no vagina?

Maybe the problem is that you neither drink nor write enough.

I always find that getting a liquor sponsor makes the entire
endeavor much more palatable.

I'm writing a news story about green funerals, and I found a graveyard online that doesn't look like a graveyard at all. It looks like a
field or a forest or something, and instead of tombstones the graves
are fitted with GPS so people can find their loved ones. A bit weird,
and doesn't make for the cool pictures, but thought you might find
it interesting.

That almost sounds like the opening of a novel. You should
keep going with it.

I have to get back to my writing—a novel about a young girl with
cancer who has the ability to communicate with ocean-dwelling
space aliens ever since she fucked her dead brother whose body
had just been shipped home from Iraq.

I can only write.
a few words.
at a time.

I've got three other novels collecting dust under my hip waders in
the basement. Three more that I literally buried, salted the earth
with, the whole nine yards.

board

I sometimes feel tempted to beat the shit out of this one guy who talks about punctuation at my bar.

I once got a semicolon pounded into my forehead by this drunken frat boy and his stupid fraternity ring.

to hell with commas
you little comma
you killer of spark and stride
know thee not that thou art
the devil's tail?
to hell with you comma
and all your cursed kin
who strike down writers in the night
who kill the letter to serve the law
you murderer of muses
who choke me with
your thistles and thickets of thorns
you bloated imp
you necrotic anti-sperm
you pregnant aborted pause
you yin longing for yang
get thee behind me comma

For the record, the lesson of this story is: Please don't defecate in a bathtub.

I'm beginning to think that there are two kinds of people in the world—those who enjoy poop humor and those who do not. I tend to embrace it, but I like to believe that my enjoyment is of the mild variety and not in any way troubling.

I once received a two-word rejection letter: "We quit." There are two ways to take that.

I think I can guess which one is correct.

Any editor who has rejected you should be ground into fine powder and sprinkled on cupcakes.

Your writing is the way I'd write if I could pick a way. You should really write a book. I mean it.

Good writers should be able to beautifully express their inability to describe something beautifully.

I think that's the story of my life: almost something. Which is a lot closer than a whole lot of nothing.

I'm just doing the same thing I've been doing for 20 years, throwing a whole bunch of shit out there and seeing what sticks to the wall. The only difference is, now stuff is really starting to stick. That'd be my advice for all the hopeless young people out there. Don't give up. Eventually, the stuff will start to stick!

What a gifted child is, in many ways, is a gifted learner. And what a gifted adult is, is a gifted doer. Those are quite separate domains of achievement.

Say you join an MFA program. Perhaps you get lucky and make a good connection. Maybe you make a major breakthrough in your style. Maybe, just *maybe,* you end up teaching. Or maybe you just owe another $40,000. Seems to me it's like the rest of what free enterprise has become: Vegas, en masse, with poor odds for you and the house winning for sure every day of the year.

I'm ashamed to admit that I have an MFA. But my shame is somewhat mitigated by the fact that I received the MFA from the University of Florida, where our motto was: "We don't give a fuck how they do it in Iowa."

Imagine if we didn't sit around a table in some dated campus building for workshop. I've found that, removed from the trappings of academia, students tend to be more motivated and more invested in the work.

My MFA writing professors didn't seem like teachers in the traditional sense. They didn't so much teach as they did, well, *show up*. It's like they were getting paid just to be present.

Is anyone more bitter than a writing professor without tenure?

Today my writing professor taught class drunk.

The only thing I ever got out of my MFA was that it made me write a lot. I think that was valuable, for what it's worth. But I had to read the writing of a lot of shitty people while I did it.

Shitty writers or shitty people? Or both?

John Gardner told his students that becoming a writer didn't require a formal education. Only the ability to educate yourself.

I don't know why I ever cared so much about learning, about education. My parents weren't educated. My mom read a lot, as did Dad, but they both lived fulfilling lives sans proper educations. The concept of school meant so very little to them.

Stay away from college instructors at all costs. Most college professors are nothing more than guides. They guide people who don't have the commitment to guide themselves.

College is the proving ground for generations of hacks, flacks, smear artists, and hatchet men. They learn how to fight dirty—and successfully counter dirty tactics—before they're out of knee pants.

Writing feels so solitary to me. Lunatic ramblings, the tremendous amount of slow, deadening time between the lunatic ramblings, and then publication. Eternal sleep in the heap of unpublished work.

Are we alone because we write, or do we write because we're alone?

Writing helps life pass by quickly.

There's nothing that can happen after a book is published that is anywhere near the rush of writing the thing.

> Right. It's like, would a straight man rather have really great sex with an average-looking woman in private, or go out on a public date with a knockout — but not be able to so much as touch her?

>> The post-publication stuff is like a public date with the knockout. The writing is the hot sex in private. There's not even a debate.

Endings always come to me after the fact. After I've stopped writing, after I've put the story away, unfinished. Or, at best, inadequately finished.

In spite of everything I shall rise again. I will take up my pencil, which I have forsaken in my great discouragement, and I will go on with my writing. If anything, I must always go on.

Work your ass off until you're too exhausted and too discouraged to go on. Then work twice as hard.

… and if I go down I shall go in flames for what other way is there to go?

> fists up
> in granite anger
> singing
> i shall not go gently into that fiery night
> levity be damned

This morning my favorite bookstore burned to the ground, my Costco. My life will never be the same.

That interests me most, as a writer. The way people find ways to hit the balls that are pitched their way, no matter the count.

Quit saving those damn rejection letters. Unless they've got some substantive editorial insight, throw the fuckers away!

Don't lose sight of why you're putting yourself through all of the labor and suffering and isolation. If you're doing it to be published, congratulations: You're a douchebag.

If you're doing it because you have to, because you feel the compulsion to articulate the oftentimes inarticulate, if you're doing it to inspire yourself, and to try and make sense out of the senseless, to rush at unseen truths for the sake of understanding, well, then, eventually you'll break through, if you work hard enough.

"Eventually" may mean 15 years, two failed marriages, and no dental insurance.

It could mean driving around town in some broke-dick Datsun, dragging your bumper. It could mean eating a lot of fish sticks.

If you want to change the world, the way to do it is not through politics or legislation. Those are just constructions. What you have to do is change the mores. And the best way to do that is through technology and art.

The worst political operatives on both sides lose their souls in the pursuit of power and influence.

One reading of Machiavelli explains that even the good guy has to deceive the public and feign religious sentiment in order to achieve good things. But ultimately it's always about power.

Basically: Screw the other guy before he screws you.

The Golden Rule: He who has the gold makes the rule.

All of my favorite bookstores are closed.

Watching the Costco burn down, I was reminded of you and your writing.

There are some people who do not go well with breakfast. You are one of those people. This is not necessarily a bad thing.

You know, reading this, I felt kind of stupid. But I guess it was worth it.

Anything could have happened. And I suppose in a way that's how it always is.

All neuroses are welcome here. We are an equal opportunity neurotic employer.

This is making my eyes cross. I think I'm seeing things. I've had to tilt my screen back and forth to be sure the words are really there.

I was here and I read this? I was here and I read this.

I'm sitting here like a boob, at my desk, trying to decide what to do next. I mumble something under my breath and dive back into my work. The office has eyes, and they bore through the circumference of my head, all 24 sets of them. I try to ignore the burn of being stared at. I try to resist refreshing the comment board. When I can no longer stand the tension I spin around in my chair and face my coworkers, and hear their collective gasp.

All writers are messengers of one kind or another. Here, the message was grave, eloquent, and *painful*, in the noblest sense possible. Probably the most poignant and selfless story anyone could ever imagine reading.

You've got to self-identify as a writer. If you're at a party and someone asks you, "So, anything published?" don't start stammering and trying to save face. Just tell them to stick their thumb up their ass, and go find a cute girl or a cute guy to flirt with. Write to grow and understand and challenge yourself, not to publish.

I'm glad I took the risks and did the things I thought were right. Even if they didn't turn out the way I had hoped most of the time.

I have 497 things to say about what you wrote. Each thing would take me 14 pages apiece.

You're beautiful and your work is poignant.

Your work has the depth of a corndog.

I'm bored to tears.

I wish I could take away all your sadness.

Do we always have to write about ourselves? Our very, very important selves. Our neurotic self-flagellating selves.

   Quite frankly, there are one too many id stories cheapening
   the sight.

      Correction: I meant to write *site*.

Your male aggregate writing size has filled me with a hard wili-
ness. I'm left strangely satisfied.

   I love the way you write about dicks and stuff like that.

      You're much bigger than you think you are.

         If anyone tells you size doesn't matter they are lying
         to your face.

            I feel a whole lot better now. I raise my glass of
            gas station wine to you.

I liked this, but I did not love it.

It's got all the trademarks of an amateur: faulty logic, vague details, unclear pronouns, lack of subject-verb agreement, misappropriation of the hyphen, zero historical context, and total insanity.

Reading this felt like a stiff kick to the nuts.

A screaming missile heard from way across the ocean. Caught in the crosshairs, totally unawares. Too late to run.

Well, I'm just happy that you don't have any lumps. I'm also happy you're a superb writer, have a gorgeous neck, and are a talented silverware balancer. But don't listen to anything I say. If you had a cancerous growth on your face, I'd lie and tell you it brings out your eyes.

If I could only swim across the ocean and thank you for telling me that.

It must've taken balls to write this.

Balls, indeed, swinging gaily toward unending bliss.

The mere thought makes me want to leave my room and find someone to fall in love with — simply to experience a tenth of the emotion present here.

This most certainly is
rhetorical catharsis.

So funny, I nearly
wet myself.

I'm always entranced by your work. I never know how to respond.
The way your words flow together makes me wish I were a better
writer.

I liked, in particular, the words.

It's your turn to be the cautionary tale.

How does it feel to be a young lion?

Who would've ever thought that a piece on one's dental history
could be so fun to read!

Your prose is something. Your dentist, however, is a moron.

Cheers to the realization that even we dentists can sometimes be morons.

It feels like if I comment on the things I like it won't be as special
as it is. So, I'll keep what I'm feeling to myself. I won't comment.

I'd love to be able to articulate a comforting or insightful reply. What this transmitted to me! But I think whatever I try to say would simply pale in comparison. I'll not ruin the moment by writing anything at all.

A comment worth making.

Envy, so much of it, coursing through your body. I bet you skipped over large chunks of this story because you knew how much it would hurt to read them.

What you just wrote, it speaks volumes of your character.

Or lack thereof.

I'm crying at work. I never cry at work.

Anybody who cries about the shackles of their ethnicity, about how it prevents them from doing this or that, is full of shit. My wife's dad used to say to her that in her lifetime, there was going to come a point when being ethnically diverse was an absolute plus. That it was always going to make you interesting. In a crowded, capitalistic world, I am an instant difference.

I am weird and strange and difficult in ways that go way beyond the ethnicity of my parents.

Welcome! It's good to finally see another young non-Caucasian here. Say, are you married?

Thanks. It feels a little less lonely in Angstville right now.

Print this out and commit it to memory.

This is the one I'll chant in the streets and parks when I'm old and crazy and have forgotten where I live.

This is the one I'll recite to all the fat nurses. To all the whipped peaches. I love fat nurses. Wandering-eyed fat nurses.

I'm a huge fan of tangents. My favorite smell is that of my dog's foot pad.

Mine is my father's body odor after a long day's work.

My mother is a fat nurse.

You're shining so brightly I can't even make out your tits.

A gem. A work of art. Unappreciated by boorish yahoos.

My God, your height and vocabulary. Striking!

We're not perfect. And no way are we going to pretend we are.

You're perfect. Exactly as you are.

There's all kind of things I could write. But I can't think of a damn thing to say. Everything there is to say has already been said.

Parts of the world simply aren't ready for you yet. But that's the price you pay for being an advanced being.

Your words dance in a rhythm I wish I could keep time with.

This was sad. It hit me in a real hard place. Your words are so beautiful and so meaningful. So devastatingly human.

This is the greatest piece of writing on handjob self-denial I have ever read.

    I don't understand most of these comments. I don't think this was very professional at all. I didn't edit it much or go back to delete anything superfluous. It's more like a blog post. I mean, I don't blog, but you know what I'm trying to say.

        It's a point of entry and it's a way for people to engage with you.

            At least people care enough about you to comment.

                Your paranoiac tendencies are delightful. For us, if not for you.

My anus is smiling right now.

My anus is laughing hard.

My one free hand raises my coffee cup in your honor.

I hope many will read this, look over their shoulders, and listen to the shadows lurking beside them.

Ultimately, we become a part of what we view. What you are looking at responds to the process of looking.

Yes, you're right—feedback works well, helps shape us as writers. It also helps form a more solid sense of spirit and community, which is all that matters at the end of the day.

Good for you for finding fun people who appreciate poop stories and good burps. Nothing worse than spending your days with people who are easily offended.

I love it when something has my name written into it. Makes me feel all mushy inside.

It was fun to read about your imminent downfall. I'm now considering slitting my wrists.

Please tell me exactly what you did.

With this, the rest of my life is suddenly so clear to me now.

I thought about leaving you a really strange and incoherent comment, as if I were tripping balls, sitting right behind you on an airplane, talking to the imaginary pilot who is wearing a hamster fur coat. But I didn't want you to think I was making fun of you.

I'm actually really stoned right now. And tripping over the weather with my best friend. I like feeling all smudged and blurry.

No comment.

Maybe I did just get dragged through hell's gravel road backward.

What the fuck am I going to do now?

> First and foremost, you need to take care of you. Educate yourself every day. Don't worry about anybody else. Never, ever worry about anybody else.

> > You might say we are creating enemies faster than we can kill them.

Unable to learn, interpret, analyze, share, and—ultimately—provide fair and constructive feedback in a group discussion.

Look, listen, learn. Stop, drop, and roll. Shake, rattle, and roll.

Listen big and talk small.

Good-bye, everyone. And thank you for reading my work.

I was here. I read this. I wrote on it, too.

Is there really only one author?

I hope this doesn't find its way into my dreams tonight.

community
desperate
other
people's
problems
writing
online
times
age
posting
essays
staring at
considering the future
going outside
wonder
the monitor
discussion
subject
matter
social networking
pcm
insulting
comments
blogging
fear of
answers
googling
context
complimentary
comments
cliches
offering criticism
yourself
opinion
moral
obligation
at a loss for words

everyone wants to be bigger than time

I'm sure everyone has Googled themselves at one time or another. But I find myself feeling a bit down when I learn about how successful the other people with my name are.

The first time I Googled myself I was working at my college newspaper. Another girl with my exact same name came up, and she worked at her college newspaper, at Yale. I was *so* disappointed in myself. She went on to become a reporter in New York City.

Oh boy, New York City, autumn time. Changing leaves. Cold-hands-hot-coffee-warm-cup. I miss New York City so bad.

I've discovered more than a couple of Googlegangers, and they're all younger and more athletic than me. This is slightly depressing.

Whenever I find another me I feel sorry for them. Inexplicably, I feel superior to them. I pity them for sharing my name but not being me. It's awful to think, but it's true. And then I wonder:

Do they feel the same way when they find out I exist?

How dare someone be almost but not quite me.

My name has been used in a byline for several bizarre porn websites. If you Google my name you will find about three that specialize in wet hairy dirty fat sweaty girly parts.

Internet Rule #34 states: "If you can imagine it, there is porn of it online."

FREE NUDE BLOND DOLL SUCKING MONSTER COCK CLOSE-UP! FREE TEEN BABES PUSSY WATER SQUIRTING TOYS!

Now imagining experimental aquatic masturbation.

There is always so much more than what we see on the surface.

I've spent many hours contemplating the relationships I've formed through my online writing. How real they are. How real I want them to be.

I have clients carrying on positively consuming relationships with people they've never met before. They are coming to me in hopes of sorting them out but I'm experiencing the same problem.

I thoroughly enjoy posting on websites, but I'm actually getting quite sick of seeing myself on the Internet.

I don't come here everyday just to see my own monkey face. I come for acute observations and droll stories, too.

I come here to preach to the choir.

I read somewhere that the best way to fight off the winter blues is sunlight, exercise, and writing a little bit on a blog every day.

Turn down the heat and slip on an itchy sweater.

Bike to work, even though it's blizzarding outside.

People journaling in public places make me grossly embarrassed for everyone in the room.

How do people find time for social networking?

A lot of people put on their best face all the time. I don't. I can't.

We are all becoming more isolated from each other as technology engenders the formation of these amorphous cyber-relationships in lieu of real, organic experiences with other people.

Through my own symbological studies, I have discovered that Facebook is actually a mind-control device that has very nearly ensnared the entire world.

MySpace and Facebook, these are much more fun if you're single.

So are strip clubs with performing dwarfs.

I got addicted to social networking because we moved away from the city, where most of my friends and family live, out to a dreadfully boring suburb in the middle of fucking nowhere, where I have nothing in common with everyone. Social networking has saved my life.

Social networking is so popular because it fills one specific need—the need for human interaction.

A 14-year-old boy in Columbus, Ohio, just Googled your name.

Before automobiles and cubicles, people interacted naturally with their community. Now we're isolated for long stretches of time, and social networking websites provide the interaction we're all longing for.

What we used to call the third place.

What we now unwittingly experience as the third mind.

I'd like to know where all the serial killers who aren't psychopathic hang out.

Friends seem so distant. I feel utterly disconnected. Relationships have taken strange turns. My lover keeps a weirdo in her cupboard.

He's Google-imaging you. Nothing's showing up.

I'm a Web 0.0 kind of girl. I have absolutely no idea about anything of which you speak here.

That's quite a way to ruin a thread, dear.

I can recall this one particular website I came across back when I was 14, when the Internet was new. You would write a letter to yourself, and then it would send it to your email at some point in the distant future. I still haven't received whatever it was I wrote to myself.

He's just done a White Pages search on you. He's found an address attached your name. You haven't lived there for several years. He looks up the address on Google Maps and looks at the address on Street View. You're nowhere in the picture. The entire street looks people-less, all peaceful and quiet.

What bothers me most about the culture at present is how many letters we're losing to email, to texting, to other electronic means of communication. I try to save my emails, but it's not the same as having an actual box full of letters.

I think it's part of the reason I look forward so rabidly to mail delivery.

I'm sending you a field of flowers.

I'm reading your work in my clean, crisp, white coat. But I'm not wearing anything underneath.

Right now I'm writing to you naked. I gotta say it feels great.

I'm in my sweatpants in my living room way the fuck out in the woods on an island, a beer by my side.

I'm huffing smog in Hollywood.

I'm ovulating right now.

Nowhere in our existence does such a place exist that is so full of lies and deception. Not even a singles bar.

This website's ethos has always been anarchy, more or less. Contributors are encouraged to tell their stories, whatever they are. And if that includes politics, opinions, or reactions to current events, then fine. If not, that's fine, too.

This site is wholly contributor created. Rules included.

I have been contemplating leaving the website. I can envision a future when it no longer exists. There was a time before it, and there will be a time after it. But right now I cannot leave.

It is what it is.

And how would one leave a website anyway? You can't. Not ever.

I could easily have cancelled my presence, but I could not have so easily cancelled all the feelings that the website has stirred up in my heart.

I'm just doing my part in the government plot to ruin the lives of everyone here.

I'm a bad reader.
I did not click on your link.
I hate it when my readers don't click on my links.
I pay in humiliation.
I'm sorry.

There is no website, there is no website, there is no website.

We operate with nothing but the things that do not exist—lines, planes, divisible time, divisible space.

How can explanation even be possible when we first make every-thing into an image, into our own image?

So we beat on, boats against the current, borne back ceaselessly into the past, on this prison planet, offering little acidly indoctri-nating pretensions and protecting them like centipedes wrapped around our precious egg masses.

One day we'll get ours.

> 185 years from now we will all be immortalized in wax in the Bangladesh Nervous Breakdown Wax Museum.

Sadly, amnesia has completely wiped out the first 28 years of my life. My earliest memory is sitting in front of a computer screen typing a message in a large box. What does POST mean?

This has been better than pulling a row of cherries on a slot machine.

These quotes have been taken utterly out of context. I won't waste my time explaining how.

Overall, your comments are not inherently insulting but rather are made insulting because it seems that to insult is your intention. I attribute that to wording. If I am wrong, then I am wrong.

Discussions like these remind me of that scene from *Monty Python's Life of Brian*, where they're sitting around, talking about what to do, but then never actually doing anything.

As a populist, I find this whole endeavor completely distasteful.

Generally speaking, people are mostly disappointing.

You're most certainly able to turn almost anything into a complaint.

Despite all the evidence proving contrary, human beings are monsters.

My readership. My servant, my friend, my foe. There to help, there to hurt. A plaything, a punching bag. A pot to piss in.

I hate feeling stupid and looked down upon. If I want that I can just go to my mother-in-law's house.

Rule #1: Never end a post with "Sorry this is so lame."

I think I get your angle. With a few thankful exceptions, you think we're all a bunch of Wallace and Lydia Davis wannabes, sullying the site with our lack of social conscience and sense of obligation to the less fortunate. Unfortunately, I think you're wrong. A goodly portion of the pieces here are quite political, but subversively rather than overtly so.

Your mocking tone does nothing to inspire any genuine creativity and/or insight. You're like the parent who thinks hitting a child will teach him not to hit others. You're exactly like your ridiculous students, and that is why they infuriate you. Their fraudulence reminds you of your own.

My students think I have X-ray vision.

You didn't think I would give up, did you? I read your email, calling my comments "off-sides," "in remarkably poor taste," and "intensely antagonistic." Then you labeled my comments "vague" and "lost to poor wording." I had a nice Christmas. Did you?

In the future I would suggest that if you wish to offer criticism, you should do so directly to those who offend you, rather than unleashing it upon the website at large.

I bet you wish I were a recluse.

It is an opinion unique to intellectuals that writers have some moral obligation to change the world.

Gee, how original.

Indeed, if the liberal arts department hadn't filled my brain so full of useless theory and other tedious garbage, I would not be partaking of this conversation, and not because I couldn't but rather because I simply wouldn't give a shit.

I'm a total snob. Not an intellectual snob or a snob about class or social status. But definitely a snob about culture and aesthetics. There's no shame in being persnickety.

A plumber, for example, would never be capable of appreciating a conversation like this.

> I know more than a few plumbers. They all make far more money than I do, and they are perfectly capable of appreciating anything and everything that's been said here. It is intellectualism — that thing that is, by definition, a disjunction between one's social and personal lives — that they would not waste their time with.

All those years spent trying to hoard as much good stuff as my mind space would allow.

I don't know that I'll ever be cultured.

There's a lot to know. And there's a lot it seems you can never know.

I want mindlessness.

I want efficiency without remorse.

I want a full-color picture menu.

I want clichés.

Pickles are nothing without the pickle juice.

I wanted to become a journalist, to try to get the word out. That didn't work. Now I don't know what I want.

I have to do something. My psychotherapist cannot be trusted. I need to get rid of her before she gets rid of me.

I've just embarked on dealing with my depression. I've been mostly unaware for far too long.

I left my apartment to see what all the fuss was all about. I took pictures, stopped and asked people questions, took a nap precisely where I shouldn't have.

> I remember lying in the street, yelling slogans at the people passing by, swinging signs, shouting obscenely loudly into an atmosphere of decline.

Some vapid, uncultured, ignorant little chippie writes down all her travails and cultural misunderstandings overseas and decides it'd be a good idea to blast them across the Internet. Life as a nanny in France. So what.

> Go the fuck home already. Paris has way too many of you dull, cookie-cutter, vacuous airhead Americans who think you're experiencing something no one else has.

> > Anyhow, you are way too hot to be obsessing over this stupid crap.

I do not understand why you included the photo of the bikini-clad girl in hip boots standing midstream holding a fishing pole. How does that fit anywhere into this?

Is it bad to admit that the only reason I began reading this was because of the titillating picture of you at the very top?

That's one way to deal with stress and anxiety: by looking at tits. The writing's good, sure, but let's be real — gratuitous shots of nipples are the reason everybody's here.

I was hoping for more pictures of your arse.

Never trust people with perfect teeth. Or perfect boob jobs.

You couldn't possibly be more unremarkable if you tried.

Here we welcome opinions on the writing, but insulting the writer is petty and boring, so fuck off.

I would never be so bold as to presume that I've made an impact on anyone's life.

Everybody hates you. Why don't you find a cave to go live in and leave everyone the hell alone?

You should thank Al Gore for inventing the Internet so you can have a place to post your shitty shit.

You seem to assume a lot about me as a person. All I've done is criticize something you've written. Grow a pair and admit that discourse over work isn't necessarily discourse over the person who wrote the work.

Where is the sign that says these comment boards are for flattery only, a meeting place where contributors can come and stroke each other's egos?

I don't know what to make of this. It's very self-indulgent and just goes on and on. We get some nice insights, here and there, but we never get the sort of dialogue that this at first promises. I suppose you could say this is a blog, and like most blogs its great failing point is that the form requires no discipline or finesse in terms of structure, audience awareness, and authorial accountability.

There seems to be a uniformity of subject matter on this website. Crotches, rectums, scrotums, phalluses, drugs, alcohol, fornication, and feces seem to be the main topics and attention grabbers, and are mercilessly piled upon us, the members of the audience. Perhaps this is how it was intended. I don't know.

There's something wrong with you. I think it's sick. It's sick, and so are you, and so is everyone else on this board. I think you're a manic depressive, and I think you're suicidal, and I think you need to seek professional help.

Seems everyone is a little sensitive about a smidgeon of crit-icism. It was obviously well deserved since it struck a chord, and, as they say, only the truth hurts.

Not every story is milk and honey and puppy dogs.

A writer isn't doing her job unless she's getting hate mail or cease-and-desist orders.

Behind all this cynicism lurks a deeper hunger for the universal truths.

If you truly love something you always look for ways to make it better.

I go out of my way to protect people here. Even strangers, which many of us are.

I think I was sincere in this. And I'm not a fundamentalist Chris-tian or a politician. I wouldn't even call myself a writer.

I believe it's possible to be sincere without being a politician or a fundamentalist Christian. Or a writer.

The word *sincere* doesn't mean anything to me. It is merely an abstraction.

My suggestion: Instead of spending time worrying about your neighbors or your girlfriend's apartment, go have great sex. Go learn a language. Travel a bit. Meet people. Let go of the angst. It's exhausting for everybody around you. Close your laptop and—oh, I don't know—be happy or something.

SNAP OUT OF IT! CUT THE MELODRAMA AND GO HAVE SOME FUN!

You might die of a heart attack at age 55.

It's nothing personal. Just par for the course.

I wonder how intelligent you really are if you have nothing better to do than spend an entire afternoon looking for spelling errors on buildings. And then write about it on the Internet.

As co-owner of the restaurant of which you bitch, I could give a shit less about the spelling or the misuse of an apostrophe. It's a logo! I can spell it or make it look however the fuck I want to because it's my business and my sign and I've paid for it. So as long as it attracts customers, what's the big deal?

My restaurants [*sic*] packed every night. So why don't you use your time a little more wisely and put your ball's [*sic*] where your mouth is and open your own business SMART GUY and put all the fucking apostrophes you want in the name. Maybe you can call it DICK-HEAD'S! HA HAHA!

I have to admit: I've had the soup there, and it's pretty good.

I don't know, man. Every time I've had an opportunity to be alone with soup I've defiled it.

Maybe if you got a real fucking job you wouldn't be so bored and do things like that.

Jobs don't relieve boredom. This much I do know.

God, we could all use a little something to cheer us up in the middle of this bitchy rampage, no?

I was offered a management position with Del Taco in June of 1997, out in Henderson. Thank God I didn't take it. I probably would've never met any of you.

I've got an idea! Let's throw a job-quitting party!

I think we can all agree that spitting openly and publicly with no regard for where it lands is hardly the same as spitting into a garbage can, or into one's own sink.

Perhaps I wouldn't be so against spitting if it weren't for all the coagulating mucus and saliva on the city streets. Why not deposit said expectorant into a tissue and toss it in the trash? You don't have to swallow it and the rest of us don't have to worry about phlegm on the soles of our shoes.

I hate smoking, but if I were in Spain, I'd smoke. The Spanish can make smoking look so cool. The Spanish and rural Kentuckians.

Spain without cigarettes seems like Los Angeles without breast implants.

No one really cares about anyone else's problems unless (a) they're fucking the person with the problems; (b) they're a family member; (c) you're a nun or a humanitarian.

I don't really mind revealing anything about myself. I'm almost pathologically driven to open up and tell everyone everything. It's probably a huge problem, but I haven't seen any consequences yet. I must have a high threshold for exposure.

I think you can count seven people who read your column.

And age doesn't matter? Then why do writers keep the same youthful photographs on their dust jackets?

You haven't gone wuss. Unless, by "wuss" you mean seeming enlightened about pretty much everything.

Sure, I'm only 27, but I've probably done three times what you've done in your 40-some-odd years on this planet.

I think people don't like to consider the future for the simple fact that anything could change in the blink of an eye. The past is done and therefore unchanging. It's easier to remember the things we've done than to try and think about the things we might do.

I don't have much advice on how to survive in the future. What do I know? I am starting to believe that the best way to exist is to try and make your own reality as small as possible.

Babble on. I mean that in the most endearing sense. Spit it out while you can. Spill your guts. Life really is too short.

And (supposedly) the Internet is forever.

Sometimes I think we should get rid of pennies altogether. Then I think I'd miss pennies. Think how much luckier we'd feel finding pennies if there weren't so many in circulation.

I wonder why you're thinking so hard about pennies.

You sound insane.

I think dents give a car character. I cherish mine.

A postpartum depressive camel is something I would like to see.

Desperate times always produce the best art.

Tell me — when are times not desperate?

It's nearly afternoon, and I haven't run into any bears. Haven't been kidnapped by terrorists. Haven't been tortured at Guantanamo. Haven't been tarred and feathered. Haven't been sodomized with a broom handle.

It's warm outside and the birds are chirping.

You suffer because you long for permanence and there is no permanence.

Everybody wants to be bigger than time.

You've crossed many waters to be here. You've drunk from the fountain of innocence, and experienced the long cold wintry years. And yet you remain the brightly burning candle in the cathedral of peace.

I wonder a lot about where all this is headed. I'm not sure how long we can keep this up. What is it leading to, culturally speaking?

I'm afraid of the answer.

For those who have fought for it, freedom has a taste the protected will never know.

I just drank a Diet Coke that tasted like an American flag purchased from a mini-mart. I feel much more patriotic now.

I remain a big fan of wonder.

There was not a single word that could've been edited from this whole thing and not a single word that could've been added.

This was something I could have done without.

I believe I'm in the vast majority when I say that this entire venture is scaring the absolute shit out of me.

Is it my imagination or is there a hidden subtext here?

Had one too many drinks tonight. And now here I am, unable to sleep, an absolute zombie, staring at the monitor at three in the goddamn morning.

I'm sensing some serious heart palpitations here. I think you need to sit down, drop your head between your knees, and breathe rapidly into a brown paper bag.

The shit has hit the fan. A bunch of my co-workers came bursting into the afternoon meeting to tell us firsthand accounts. The office was skeleton-staffed that day. Nearly everyone left to join the protest.

Rioting is serious business. It is democracy in action, when people really stand up to be heard, when the people really act as the government. These people stand with nothing but their bodies and voices against high-tech weapons, against unmatchable political power. These people are more than patriotic heroes. They fight for the world.

I've felt paralyzed lately, muted by the headlines, too old to bury my head in the sand and yet too green to know really what to do.

And with all of this I still feel like I've not made one ounce of difference. Nothing has changed. Nobody cares. And I'm so, so tired.

If you'll excuse me, I'm off on my dogsled to the hospital and then the maple syrup farm.

The bad news is bad but the good news is great.

Puffs joint. Stares at plane flying overhead. Coughs.

Well, I think when it's all said and done the comments here are as valuable as the very thing they're commenting on.

To me, the comments are like tiny precious gems.

I've always loved the comments most of all.

Signing off from the land of 24-hour freedom and long-distance wars.

Fingers crossed. Extremely superstitious. Cautiously optimistic.

An excellent outcome. Was it worth your time?

I would leave a comment. But I'm at a loss for words right now.

authors' bios

Justin Benton is a writer who lives in Lexington, Kentucky.

Brad Listi is a writer and the founding editor of The Nervous Breakdown. He lives in Los Angeles.

a note on the type

The text is set in Adobe Caslon Pro. Before William Caslon cut his first typeface in 1722, English printers used Dutch type. Caslon modelled his letters on Dutch Baroque forms, but gave them more delicate lines. Caslon type spread throughout the British Empire and was used to set the 1776 Declaration of Independence. "Modern" faces like Bodoni briefly supplanted Caslon in the early 19th century, but the British Arts & Crafts movement resurrected Caslon because of the type's readability, beauty, and utility. Until the digital age, a motto among printers was, "When in doubt, use Caslon."

> The Adobe Systems digital version of Caslon was designed by Carol Twombly in 1990. In 1994 Twombly was the first woman to win the *Prix Charles Peignot*, an international award for typeface designers under 35. Twombly's other digital typeface designs include Chaparral, Lithos, Trajan, and Myriad.

The titling is set in "city burn night after night and we spraypaint the walls," a 2008 grunge/trash font by French designer Thibault Dietlin, owner of Alien Foundery.

BOOKS

*invites you to view
our catalogue of other fine titles.*

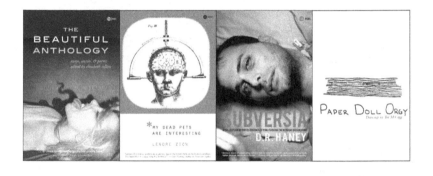

*Print editions are available
at all major online retailers,
including Amazon, Barnes & Noble,
and Powell's.*

*E-book editions are available
at all major e-book retailers,
including Amazon, the iBookstore, and BN.com.*

www.thenervousbreakdown.com

The Beautiful Anthology
edited by Elizabeth Collins

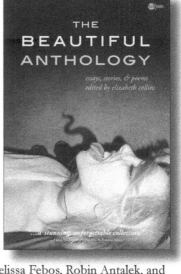

"A stunning, unforgettable collection."
—Diana Spechler
　　Author of *Who by Fire* and *Skinny*

This groundbreaking anthology of
essays, stories, and poems explores
what women and men find beautiful
in life. The answers will surprise you,
shock you, amuse you, and make you
think. The 26 contributors (including
best-selling authors Jessica Anya Blau, Melissa Febos, Robin Antalek, and
Greg Olear) form an eclectic, international compendium. Illustrated with
photographs and art. (264 pp)

My Dead Pets Are Interesting
by Lenore Zion

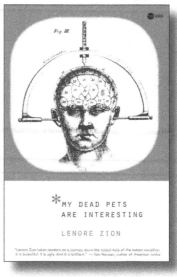

*"Zion takes readers on a journey down the rab-
bit hole of the human condition. It is beautiful.
It is ugly. And it is brilliant."*
—Tom Hansen
　　Author of *American Junkie*

*"The most disquieting, surprisingly poignant
and shockingly honest stories you will ever do
yourself the favor of reading."*
—Kimberly M. Wetherell
　　Award-winning filmmaker

In this hilarious collection of personal
essays, Lenore Zion offers her unique perspective on everything from
foot fungi to prep schools, day spas, and dead birds. Macabre, irreverent,
beautiful, and unsettling, *My Dead Pets* is an unimpeachably funny trip
down into the depths of Zion's mind. (228 pp)

Subversia
by D.R. Haney

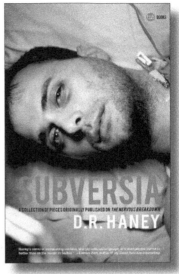

"Haney interweaves tiny details with weighty subjects deftly, through articles smartly ordered for just the right balance of thematic lilt and interest-holding lurch."
—Matt Cook, *Pank Magazine*

In this bare-knuckled, frankly autobiographical collection, D.R. Haney shares essays on his artistic struggles and evolution. Haney brilliantly dissects his wide-ranging incarnations: punk rock malcontent in 1980s New York, B-movie actor in Roger Corman films, screenwriter on *Friday the 13th: Part VII*, expatriate writer in Serbia, and author of the celebrated underground novel *Banned for Life*. *Subversia* is written with the bracing candor and lyrical beauty that have earned Haney a cult following worldwide. (240 pp)

Paper Doll Orgy
drawings by Ted McCagg

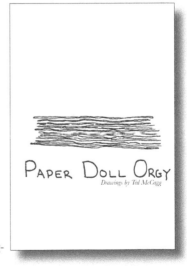

"Ted McCagg is a truly original thinker who really makes me laugh. And for that, I hate him."
—Conan O'Brien

For the first time, Ted McCagg's cartoons are collected where they have always longed to live: the printed page. His work, which has won him a legion of fans throughout cyberspace, is a regular feature on *The Nervous Breakdown* and has appeared elsewhere on the web at *The Atlantic*, *The Washington Post*, and *Laughing Squid*. (208 pp)